To Grandma Happy Christmas From Olivia

Young Writers 2005 POETRY COMPETITION

PLAYGROUND Poets

Let your creativity flow...

CW00607342

- Inspirations From Hertfordshire
Edited by Steve Twelvetree

 Young**Writers**

First published in Great Britain in 2005 by:
Young Writers
Remus House
Coltsfoot Drive
Peterborough
PE2 9JX
Telephone: 01733 890066
Website: www.youngwriters.co.uk

SB ISBN 1 84602 242 8

Foreword

Young Writers was established in 1991 and has been passionately devoted to the promotion of reading and writing in children and young adults ever since. The quest continues today. Young Writers remains as committed to the fostering of burgeoning poetic and literary talent as ever.

This year's Young Writers competition has proven as vibrant and dynamic as ever and we are delighted to present a showcase of the best poetry from across the UK. Each poem has been carefully selected from a wealth of *Playground Poets* entries before ultimately being published in this, our thirteenth primary school poetry series.

Once again, we have been supremely impressed by the overall high quality of the entries we have received. The imagination, energy and creativity which has gone into each young writer's entry made choosing the best poems a challenging and often difficult but ultimately hugely rewarding task - the general high standard of the work submitted amply vindicating this opportunity to bring their poetry to a larger appreciative audience.

We sincerely hope you are pleased with our final selection and that you will enjoy *Playground Poets - Inspirations From Hertfordshire* for many years to come.

Contents

Gemma Shipway (8)	33
Amber Forrow (7)	34
Louise Dunn (9)	34
James Perfect (7)	35
Harry McLaren (8)	35
Tom Thurlow (7)	35
Danielle Fitzgerald (9)	36
Paris Lewis (9)	36
Bradley Hoskin (8)	36
Emma Payne (9)	37
Roberto Catarinicchia (9)	37
Laura Newby (9)	37
Megan Sprake (9)	38
Rosie Sperrin (9)	38
Jason Bull (9)	39
Antony Hughes (9)	39
Bliss O'Dea (9)	39
Ellie Finch (8)	40
Conor Ward (9)	40
Emily Buckland (9)	41

Bushey Manor Junior School

Eleni Zachariou (8)	41
Max Wolf (7)	41
Michael Hague (8)	42
Kirsty Henley-Washford (9)	42
Alice Houbart (9)	43
Jacob Chase-Roberts (8)	43
Rosie Durant (9)	44
Emily Grieve (9)	44
Eve Anglesey (10)	45
Louise Warren (10)	45
Natalia Cordeiro (10)	46
Anna Chase-Roberts (10)	46
James Bernays (10)	47
Robbie Gent (9)	47
Ellie-May O'Keefe (9)	48
Leanna Joyce (8)	48
Olivia Frinton (9)	49
Keelan Naidoo (9)	49
Oron Sheldon (8)	50

Alan Sutch (9)	50
Owen Scully (9)	51
Charlotte Liebling (9)	51
Grace Desney Ellis (9)	52
Megan Fitzpatrick (9)	52
Emma Mascall (9)	53
Sarah Sharp (8)	53
Shelby Fowler (9)	54
Megan Thornton (8)	54
Amy Dolley (9)	55
Jerram Counter (8)	55
Louis Evans (9)	56
Jake Holmes (9)	56
Olivia Myrtle (9)	57
Nathan Foster (8)	57
Leo Jurascheck (10)	58
Natalie Barton (8)	58
Marium Hamid-Chohan (8)	59
Taylor Cobb (8)	59
Marianne Roe (9)	60
Emily Forrester (8)	60
Kate Good (8)	61
Zacharesh Bingham Thaker (9)	61
Reece Doyle (9)	62
Rachel South (9)	63
Jake Simmonds (9)	64

Chaulden Junior School

Patsy Milligan (11)	64
Saraya Bowlzer (11)	65
Jessica Dillon (11)	65
Rhianna Wilding (11)	66
George Gomme (11)	66
Courtney Hart (11)	66
Carrie-Anne Smith (11)	67
Poppy Haynes (11)	67
Kelly-Ann Walker (11)	67
Casey Bird (11)	68
Alice Head (11)	68
Kristy Hopkins (11)	68
Harrison Robb (11)	69

Jasmine Patel (11)	69
Siobhan Keegan (11)	69
Rachel Tofield (10)	70
Alex Radford (11)	70
Helena Simmons (11)	70
Andrew Hardwick (11)	71
Billy Stevens (11)	71
Guy Grigsby (10)	71
Edward Duell (10)	72
Barnaby Brown (11)	72
Nicole Wilks (12)	72
Corrie Seaton (11)	73
Tahnee Gavin (11)	73
Jake Caley (10)	74

Colney Heath JMI School

Emily Fox (10)	74
Olivia Goulding (10)	75
Clara Ryan (9)	75
Alexander Wells (10)	76
Zenon Sasiak Rushby (10)	76
Abbie Fox (9)	77

Eastbrook Primary School

Amber Brinson (11)	77
Iain Noble (11)	78
Claire Perreira (9)	78
Demi McGlen (8)	79
Michael Williams (11)	80
Shannon Austin (9)	80
Danny Kachouh (10)	81
Daniel Morrissey (10)	81
Lois Payne (9)	82
Jayson McGlen (11)	83
Jack Cooper & Ossie Williams (11)	84
Emma Gates & Luke Hampton (11)	84
Aisha Saeed (11)	85
Tara Morrell (11)	85
Kelly-Marie Daly (10) & Fazari Peeraullee (11)	86
Georgie-May Lancashire (11)	87
Charley Richardson (9) & Lilymay Vansittart (10)	88

Daniela Sabella (11)	89
Hope Moriarty (9)	90
Robbie Bates (10)	91
Ian Hardwick (10)	92

Fleetville Junior School

Ruqayyah Afzal (11)	92
Caroline Thomas (10)	93
Ben Rodell & Jack Hopkins (11)	93
Samuel Sharp (11)	94
Chloe Swift (11)	94
Philip Ruis (10)	94
Kieran Tidball (10)	95
Hollie Coupar (11)	95
Shona Smith (11)	96
Gail Coles (11)	96
Levi Gatfield (10)	96
Saoirse Hill (10)	97
Laura Paul (11)	97
Matthew Knight (9)	97
Claudia Cliffe (11)	98
Jojo Mills (10)	98
William Akhurst (11)	99
Jack Hopkins (11)	99
Tahiya Khatun (10)	99
Stefan Maile (11)	100
Helen Tung Yep (11)	100
Oliver Grisenthwaite (10)	100
Nell Rogers (11)	101
Frankie Dean (9)	101
Tevin Charles (11)	101
Philip Madgwick (11)	102
Aisha Khan (10)	102
Nevena Stojkov & Marina Ragusa (10)	103
Sophie Kiani (10)	103
Grace Vance (10)	104
Anna Nayler (10)	105
Kate Richardson (10)	105
Jessica Murray (11)	106
Maria Parikh (11)	106
Harriet Knafler (11)	106

Cara Lomas (10)   107
Adele Robinson (10)   107
Rachael Drane (11)   107
Anna Fordham (10)   108
John Clough (10)   108
Isabel Maile (8)   109

Gaddesden Row JMI Primary School
Dominic Attoh (7)   109
Lucy Hodson (7)   110
Adam Rowland (10)   110
Kerry Burnage (8)   111
Darren Pike (9)   111
Alfie Thackeray (8)   112
Lajor Cole-Etti (11)   112
Ami Johnson (8)   113
Jake Brown (9)   113
Chloe Wheals (8)   114
Saffron White (8)   114
Lily Highfield (10)   114
Latir Cole-Etti (11)   115
Ellen Holdsworth (9)   115

Roebuck Primary School & Nursery
Kieran Chauhan (10)   115
Tom Borcherds (8)   116
Kieran Hanrahan (9)   116
Hayley Briars (9)   117
Chloe Emmerson (9)   117
Kieran Hudson (10)   117
Chloe Grant (9)   118
Penny Johns (9)   118
Aaron Marshall (9)   118
Stephanie Noble (9)   119
Oliver Petts (9)   119
Megan Ridley (9)   119
Luke Thompson (9)   120
Kimberley Roberts (9)   120
Hayley Trudgill (10)   120
Georgia Steed (9)   121
Ashley Watson (10)   121

Emilie Cherry (11)	146
Sarah Mitchelson (11)	147
Peter De'Ath (9)	148
Emma Knowles (10)	149
Rachel Christie (10)	150
Megan McGuiness (10)	151

Sandon JMI School

Chelsea D'Arcy (10)	151
Jack Squires (11)	152
Hannah Stout (9)	152
Hannah Reynolds (9)	153
Meg Lewitt (10)	153
Connor D'Arcy (8)	154
Danielle Moon (7)	154
Faye Piggott (7)	154
James Tucker (9)	155
Rachel Croker (9)	155
Alex Close (8)	155
Callum Thomas (10)	156
Luke Mongston (11)	156
Luke Geaves (9)	157

Sheredes Primary School

Stefan Norton-Dando (11)	157
Megan Coleman (11)	157
Hollie Cooksley (10)	158
Oliver Moule (10)	158
Max Mayhew (10)	158
Marc Reed (10)	159

Stonehill School

Emma Buchanan (11)	159
Rhiannon Barry (11)	160
Ellen Millar (11)	161
Tao Haskins-Coulter (10)	162
Aiden Collins (10)	162
Hannah Daly (11)	163
Ashley Castle (10)	164
Alex Kelly (11)	165

The Poems

Buildings

As I ran down the loud, busy street,
I stopped and gawped at the towering giant right in front of me,
It towers over all the massive buildings,
The windows reflect the bright midday sun,
Blinding you every time you look,
This gigantic building must touch the sky,
The stillness of it is completely different
To the small white clouds scudding across the sky.

As I walked down the quiet, empty track,
I stopped and stared at the small, beautiful dwarf right in front of me,
It shines out like a beacon with its spectacular beauty.
The little thatched roof is neat and patterned by the rainfall,
The chimney puffs little clouds of smoke into the pale blue sky,
The tiny building with the spring flowers,
The white wall is completely different to the dark brown,
                                        wooden beams.

Rufus Talks (11)
Ashwell Primary School

The Rhino

His eyes are gloomed and droopy,
His ears prick up to hear,
His tail slaps left and right,
His teeth are slowly crunching,
His toenails are pebbles,
His skin is grey and wrinkled,
His brilliant sense of smell,
His horn all curved and battered,
So who is this delightful beast?
With the features I just said,
Can you think of no one?
A rhino of course!

Annie Price (11)
Ashwell Primary School

Going Shopping

Let's see what's in the shops today,
And work out how much I should spend,
On clothes for my new trend.

Should I buy . . .
A pretty pink primrose purse,
And a sparkling silver skirt?
Or . . .
A beautiful belt
With a pair of gem-studded jeans?
Or . . .
Stylish shimmering shoes with
Two pairs of stripy and spotty socks?
Or . . .
Some gorgeous girly gloves
And a tasteful top?
Shopping's so much fun,
If shopping was food
I'd eat it all day long.

Olivia Lohoar Self (10)
Ashwell Primary School

Summer Is Here!

Spring goes and summer is now here,
Flowers bloom and birds sing,
Because summer is here.
Children laugh as the sun shines
For summer is here.
Ice creams dribble and sandcastles grow,
Summer is here.
Birds fly through the trees,
At last summer is here.

Cara Deal (10)
Ashwell Primary School

Art

Like all your thoughts put together onto paper,
Or into a sculpture, whatever you like.
You can do it mindlessly, or with concentration all directed
                                              onto your piece
People can stop you doing most things,
But no one can stop you doing art.

Cleo King (11)
Ashwell Primary School

Friends

Friends are like family and you choose for yourselves
We tell each other our most secretive secrets
That no one could ever find out.

We play and muck about happily and crazily
All day long, and never get bored.

Friends are like family we choose for yourselves
And that you can always trust.

Charlotte Cavanagh (11)
Ashwell Primary School

Witch

W ill, a powerful wonder, element energy.
 I mam, a spontaneous spark, element water
 T oranee, a bright brain box, element fire.
 C ornelia, a flowery flutter, element earth.
 H ay-lin, an imaginative inventor, element air.
                Witch, the power of five.

Sofia Luggeri (11)
Ashwell Primary School

Fish

Morning on the river.
A pike hides from view
Waiting for its prey.
A roach swims over searching for food.
The pike darts forward and kills it so quickly.
Splash! Splash! Splash!
The morning shatters.
Birds fly off in alarm.
A normal day on the river.

Luke Jones (11)
Ashwell Primary School

Santa

Santa Claus is here.
He has a gigantic sack,
Sitting along his back.
I wonder what I've got,
Maybe a load of presents,
Or maybe a lump of coal.
Thanks Santa for a wonderful Christmas.

Rebecca Court (11)
Ashwell Primary School

My Pet

My pet doesn't have a shell
My pet does have a fin
My pet doesn't live on land
My pet does have a chin
My pet doesn't eat beans
My pet doesn't bark
For my pet is a tough, rough, mean, green . . .

Charlie Hatton (8)
Brookland Junior School

Sploshing Water

S wirling and sploshing and having so much fun
P ouring and paddling and we have just begun
L akes and rivers are so lovely too
A falling and crashing comes down on the ground
S mashing down in little bumps. What is it?
H ailstones, hailstones are glittery, sparkly, shiny too and they are so
I ce-cold when they melt, the ground is slippery
N ot as slippery as snow but still so
G lossy and glittery as hailstones.

Emma Ford (10)
Brookland Junior School

Water

W ater is great, swishing
A nd splashing
T he children playing,
E nding up staying in the water
R oar at the water, playing your game.

Ben Isaacs (10)
Brookland Junior School

Water

S wimming back and forth the lakes
W aves that go as high has stakes
I am having so much fun,
M oving slowly through the sea
M oving away from the bee
I keep on moving through the sea
N othing's going to bother me
G oing faster through the sea,
   Changing speed, oh dearie me.

Mary Fasipe (10)
Brookland Junior School

Water, Water Here And There

G ushing water here and there
L ovely water everywhere
I ce frozen on frosty days
T ides coming in across the bays
T rickling rain down the stream
E very day appears the water queen
R unning through the water
Y ou and me together forever splashing around till moonlight.

Katie Jones (10)
Brookland Junior School

Rushing Water

T ides rushing in and out
R unning in rivers and lakes
I ce defrosting in the sunshine
C urrents on cold, ice days
K icking and splashing, dripping and dropping
L ashing and creeping the waves they go
I n the rain children play
N ow where did the water go?
G lossy water, *drip, drop, splish, splash, splosh.*

Evangeline Hughes (10)
Brookland Junior School

All About Water

P eople hiding
O utside storms
U mbrellas drip drops
R iver splashing over rocks
I cy, people shiver
N o play
G urgling drain.

Molly Adams (9)
Brookland Junior School

Tsunami

T ake a bath,
S plash, splash,
U se a towel,
N o, don't get me wet,
A nd make a splash,
M ake the tsunami by your splosh,
 I s the tsunami gone yet?

Georgia O'Connor (10)
Brookland Junior School

Butterfly

Peaceful and silent,
Featherweight,
Swooping in the sunlit sky,
Flower to flower,
Tree to tree
Beautiful I can be,
I hypnotize young children,
To follow my bright and wonderful colours,
Fragile and delicate,
I fight a strong battle.

Meghan Smith (11)
Brookland Junior School

Water

W ater is hot
A nd can be cold
T hen rain comes
E asy to hold
R ivers and lakes are water!

Stevie Goddard (10)
Brookland Junior School

Disaster

S torm powerfully pulls you to the ground
P ushing and pulling struggle pulls you on the ground
L ush water sloshes round and round
A tidal wave coming down
S creaming sizzling water coming for us
H owling, screaming, the water is coming, then a silent hush!

Bradley Casey (10)
Brookland Junior School

Tsunami Disaster

T he terrible tides and raging seas,
S wirling around among the weeds
U nstoppable waves so long and deep
N ever normal just so steep
A lways moving never stopping,
M agnificent waves always dropping
I ncredible water can also never return.

Katie Millard (10)
Brookland Junior School

Tsunami

T ragic tides and rapid rivers,
S tormy seas that make me quiver.
U nimaginable waterfalls and mighty crashes,
N ippy currents and winds that dash
A mazing noises and wild waves
M agical treasures hidden in the caves
I nteresting sights to see!

Shannen Gray (10)
Brookland Junior School

Water

T is for turtles swimming beneath the sea
S is for sharks eating people alive
U is for underneath the deep, dark sea
N is for Nan's sunbathing under the sun
A is for animals having all kinds of fun
M is for Mum's sleeping on a lilo
I is for impossible to hit your brother with a water gun.

Aaron Demeyer (10)
Brookland Junior School

Tidal Wave

Water is running down lakes
Everybody comes and says
'What an amazing tidal wave'
Everybody said to me
'Can I drink the river please?'

Luke Ciccone (10)
Brookland Junior School

Wacky Water

W acky water is really fun, it keeps you cool in the sun!
A nyone can get wet even if you're someone's pet!
T iny droplets of water can be good but most people wear a hood!
E ven water can be bad, a boy went swimming and it killed the lad!
R unning water is really cool but even better is a swimming pool!

Andrew Isaacs (10)
Brookland Junior School

Water

Thunder, lightning, raining storms
Crash! Bang! The temperature forms
Running water rushing down
Oh no! The tsunami has hit the town
Iceberg, iceberg run away
Split, splat, splosh today
Cold as it may be, swimming is still fun
We can play, laugh and run!
Kick, splash in the puddles,
Let's get round and make a huddle
Laughing, loudly in the sun
The children are having so much fun
I love waterfalls swirling blue
I am going to wet you
Now where did the water go?
It's evaporated, condensation, precipitation, oh!
Green waves hit the rocks,
Crash! Bang! Against the blocks!

Ruby Lacey (10)
Brookland Junior School

Water, Water

W ater water
A nimals drink it, water, water
T eachers drink it, water, water
E lliot drinks it, water, water
R ain is water.

Elliot Forte (10)
Brookland Junior School

Good And Bad Things About Water! Haiku

Water is rushing
When it comes gushing in fast
Run for your life, go!

George Ansell (9)
Brookland Junior School

The Sea Is Crashing - Haiku

The sea is crashing
The waves are washing - don't run
The crashing seas calm.

Perry Fordham (10)
Brookland Junior School

The Sea - Haiku

The huge sea waves crash
Against the shore like thunder
And the waves ripple.

Luke Robinson (10)
Brookland Junior School

The Waterfalls

The waterfalls are whizzy
Rushing down the hard bumpy rocks
Into the azure river.

Charlee Buckingham (9)
Brookland Junior School

Silky Waves - Haiku

The swift wild water
With great azure silky waves
Flying down the drains.

Chloe Rennick (9)
Brookland Junior School

The Sparkling Stream - Haiku

The stream trickles down
Chilly, sapphire liquid,
Calming, clean and pure.

Helen Perry (9)
Brookland Junior School

Swimming

The dripping soft warmth
To splash and get wet
Play in it with your very own pet.

Ellie-Lee McLaren (10)
Brookland Junior School

Dashing Water - Haiku

The sea was bolting
The ocean was dashing fast
The paddles splashed wild.

Tyler Silverosa (10)
Brookland Junior School

Zooming Sea - Haiku

The sea was zooming
It was like a thunderstorm
The sea was shocking.

Serhat Sezgin (10)
Brookland Junior School

Sparkling Water - Haiku

Water is sparkling
Water is swishy and fun
Water is the best.

Jadene Cook (10)
Brookland Junior School

The Shimmering Sea!

Crisp sapphire sea
Wild splashing water
Roaring drops like lions.

Katie Sweet (9)
Brookland Junior School

Waterfall - Haiku

Sapphire water
Tearing down onto the rocks
Freely flowing off.

Drew Wickenden (10)
Brookland Junior School

Magic

A black hooded cloak,
Ancient as the Earth,
Waving his wand at his side,
Magic.

Most powerful wand in the world,
Casting spells everywhere,
The wand is extremely powerful
It is as powerful as a marvellous magician.
Magic.

The thunder, lightning,
A storm is brewing
In the angry sky,
Raining extremely hard,
Flooding a nearby village,
Magic.

Wand is too powerful,
Then he is lying still,
Then death,
In seconds,
Everything went silent,
Magic.

Lauren Hoskin (10)
Brookland Junior School

Water Sounds And Looks - Haiku

Bright shimmer of rain,
Blinding dazzle of calm seas,
The roaring of waves.

George Clark (10)
Brookland Junior School

The Cave

A cave of laughing heads,
A deadly beast waits
A cunning plan baits
Hiding in the water
The tentacled terror waits.

In a cave of loss and doom,
A book awaits destruction
Pain will be dispersed.

A cave of laughing heads,
A deadly beast waits,
A cunning plan baits,
Hiding in the water,
The ten tentacled terror waits.

Into the caves gaping mouth,
The skeleton has awakened from a deep, deep sleep,
Death, death the stopper of life.

A cave of laughing heads,
A deadly beast waits,
A cunning plan baits,
Hiding in the water,
The ten tentacled terror waits.

Torin Adamson-Woods (10)
Brookland Junior School

The Thunderstorm - Haiku

The clashing thunder,
The silky and sparkling waves
Roaring at the shore.

Monika Rosie Young (10)
Brookland Junior School

The Horror

The magician was old as Earth,
Hooded and cloaked,
Magical,
Powerful.
Living amongst kings,
The magician was old as Earth.

The temple stands firm,
Phantoms swarm the grounds.
A book of horrors,
A book of death.

Diamonds are life.
An all-seeing eye,
Trapped.
Lost souls return,
Seeping, souring, sighing.
Diamonds die.

The magician was old as Earth,
Hooded and cloaked,
Magical,
Powerful.
Sleeping amongst kings,
The magician was old as Earth.

Rachel Prior (10)
Brookland Junior School

Waterfalls

Waterfalls are crashing
Azure water wispy and loud
Falling from the rocks.

Mitchell Tuvey (10)
Brookland Junior School

Trees

In the day a gentle soul,
Giver of shade and life,
Guard the fields,
Like sentries they do,
All hunched together.

Night comes
It turns into a monster,
Swaying and dancing,
Lashing its branches,
A whip out of control
Bare trees stretch their witches' fingers,
Grabbing its prey,
Only to feel the wind.

Morning arrives,
Soft, silent and still,
The tree is again.

Hollie Persico (11)
Brookland Junior School

Wind

A beautiful breeze that blows and flows
It stays and goes between your toes
The flowers dance in a trance
With a gentle touch but it doesn't seem much!
At night the wind might give you a fright
With its whistling and whooshing
With its fierce invisible touch,
Don't worry it's only wind, it won't hurt!

Amie Fletcher (11)
Brookland Junior School

Leaves

As wrinkled as a granny,
Smooth to the touch,
Gone in the winter,
Not that much.

Thick or thin,
Big or small
You don't get them in one size,
They come in all!

We make a good bonfire,
Making lots and lots of smoke
We crackle as we burn,
Enough to make you choke.

We have our many uses,
Like making things colourful
Especially in the autumn,
When things are dull.

Dancing in the wind,
Being split up from their friends
Racked up by the gardeners,
Not a happy end!

Charlotte Roper (11)
Brookland Junior School

Clouds

They are high against the sea-blue sky.
They cling together to stop the bullying wind.
They are swept away by aeroplanes making patterns
People stand and stare and wonder why they are so high up.
They don't come in one size, they come in all,
Some flat, some wide, some so high, you can't see them at all.

Lauren Evans (11)
Brookland Junior School

Snail

On a journey,
To prove to the world,
That he's strong.
Taking it slow,
Enjoying life.
A traveller on his own.

Slithering, sliding, snaking across the grass.
A gardener's friend,
No, a foe.
As the world is against him,
He stays to the side
Sneaking around.
Hidden.

The trail of the traveller
Gleams and glints in the daylight,
Glows and glitters in the moonlight.
Taking his home wherever he goes.

Tess O'Halloran (11)
Brookland Junior School

Bees

Buzz, buzz the bees sound
Buzzing, burning bees,
Black and yellow stripes,
Hypnotizing the mind,
Dancing in the sun in harmony,
Flying elegantly in the breeze,
Swaying in the trees
Buzz, buzz the bees go.

Gabrielle Young (11)
Brookland Junior School

Magic Locations

Silent.
Never seen,
Face not showing,
Actions wise,
Never ponders.
Magic dark
Magic for good.
In a world of his own.
Magician.

Minds of their own,
Minds confused.
Trees moving
Transfixed
Wind seed
Colours intertwining
Whizzing around.
Spells.

Flashing skies,
Floorboards creaking,
Werewolf whistling,
Fearful locations,
Graveyard zombies,
Ebony sky,
One thing only.
Death.

Jamie Wills (11)
Brookland Junior School

The Beetle

The black warrior roams the ground.
Its black armour glistens in the sun.
The weapons ready for combat.
Their enemies' tanks go into action.
They also fly over the enemies' safe and out of reach.

Mitchell Bates (10)
Brookland Junior School

Clouds

Clouds
Floating by like
Sheep with no legs
And fluffy scrambled eggs
Not always what they seem
In different shapes and sizes
And sometimes in your dreams.

Summer fades
Day by day
Winter comes.

Angry and evil
Fierce and grey
With thunder and lightning
Appear rather frightening
Moaning and groaning
Trees tremble with fear
Stay in your houses
Away from out here,
Clouds.

Jodie Mackay (11)
Brookland Junior School

My Pet

My pet has long ears
My pet can fly
My pet has a little head
My pet can't wave goodbye
My pet eats leaves
My pet doesn't wear a hat
For my pet is a frightful, delightful,
Speedy,
Weedy
Blind
And
Brave . . .

Sarah White (9)
Brookland Junior School

Twigs

Twigs are just not tough to us
But to ants they are so strong,
Some are nice and some are not
Like plain sticks with thorns.

As strong or tough you think it is
It has its own weakness,
Like a fire or boy if you ever see a twig
Don't use it as a tiny toy.

Snap, snap is all you hear
When a fire is near,
Strong as a wall or as weak as a fly
But small like a fly
Snap, snap, snap the end is near.

Ryan Boldick (11)
Brookland Junior School

Magic

A dark-hooded cape
Lies around his neck.
As dark as night,
As old as Earth,
Powerful and magical.

Slowly sparks begin to fly,
From the forceful wand.
Then after that
Enormous forks of lightning,
Powerful and magical.

Then suddenly a terrifying battle is fought.
Leading to silence and stillness,
No longer powerful and magical.

Megan Bloomfield (11)
Brookland Junior School

The Quest

Dark-hooded.
Standing.
Waiting
For his tribe.
Sparks shooting everywhere.

Killer book.
Sitting.
Wanting to kill.
Waiting for deadly spirits.
Destroying the world.
Only one will sacrifice.
Themselves
To stop the
World from being destroyed.
But which one?

Lying on the floor.
Blood pouring.
No one there
Except for one.
Covering the penetrating body
All because of the deadly book.

Olivia Keown (11)
Brookland Junior School

Clouds

Sheepish clouds drifting across summer's sky,
Fluffy like candyfloss,
White as snow,
Silently, silently they drift
Making faces as they go.

Kirby-Rose McIntosh (11)
Brookland Junior School

A Quest

Wizards seeking,
The Diamond of Life.
Held in a temple of all puzzles
Quest
A quest is what he'll go on.

Gates
Approaching gates
Wizards consider
Gingerly picking the right gate
To enter.

Halls
Hall of spirits
Ghastly voices
Blood stains shine
From the reflection of
The Diamond of Life.

Successfully the quest
Ends.
It is over . . . or is it?

Reece Watson (11)
Brookland Junior School

Fence

Big strong soldiers guarding your territory,
Stand tall and proud,
Outlining your boundaries,
Even though graffiti swarms over them,
Like a permanent rash,
Turning them into ugliness,
They still are protective,
Stay there and guard your fortress.

Emily Sprake (11)
Brookland Junior School

Death

Ancient as Earth.
Standing alone.
Extinct and worn out.
Overgrown cliff.
Clouds passing.
Mirror on the wall.
Reflecting.

Enemy.
Hate and dislike.
Dying in pain.
Death.
End of life.
Gone.

Katie Page (11)
Brookland Junior School

The Quest

His staff is the magician's most prized possession,
One swish and he's left his mark,
The magician is wise and old,
His hands as rough as bark.

The sun's rays fire at this mirror,
But they only come bouncing back.
The menacing mirror reflects all the colours
Ruby red, golden yellow and even ebony black.

It wanders around through the misty night,
Its precious prey not having a clue.
So next time you're out and all on your own,
Watch out.
Its next victim could be you!

Josh O'Brien (11)
Brookland Junior School

The Hero Lifts His Staff

The hero,
Lifts his staff,
Gazes around for the Kingdom of Glass.

When sailing across the seven seas he sees,
A picture of the
Kingdom of Glass.
So shiny.
So sparkly.
So magical.
The doorknob twists,
His heart thumped,
Like a drum roll.
Peering into the room,
Only a reflection is to be seen.
Who is the magician?

The hero has transformed into a king,
A great king,
The king of the Kingdom of Glass.
An old life has drifted away.

Amber Stanford (10)
Brookland Junior School

The Quest

Mysterious hooded man stood as if he had seen a ghost
Mysterious hooded man stood on a forbidden temple
Some magic words with a flash of light
The light stops.
The sunbeams shoot on a crystal clear sea
It is a golden and flat. What is it?
The sand is death!

Jack Sturgeon (10)
Brookland Junior School

The Quest

Four terrifying guards.
Two brave children.
One single death.
This is what happens.

Dark-hooded.
Magician.
Stood still
In the pelting rain.

Golden seats.
Silver archways.
Opening closing thorn doors.
Inside the temple rattling with fear.

Four terrifying guards.
Two brave children.
One single death.
This is what happened.

Charlotte Dean (11)
Brookland Junior School

The Power Of Magic

Magician so old that he looks older than the Earth.
However he is very bright and intelligent.
Magician uses magic powers to show off,
And impress.

He gazes into the mirror
He feels magical and pleased with himself.
The magician's old life was wasted,
Now he has a fresh start.

Lauren Palgrave (11)
Brookland Junior School

Seeking

Try to find,
Never seen,
But always there.
Travel far,
Seeking the one and only.
Ancient as the Earth.
Powerful as the sun,
Magician!

Bursting with power,
Never dying,
Never moving,
Never waking,
Sleeping always.
Key to all eternity.
Puzzled minds unravel.
Life of diamond here now.

As dark as midnight
Never gone
Always near.
In the air
As free as a bird
Searching for its next victims
Blood-curdling thoughts of death.

Bethany Jones (11)
Brookland Junior School

Epitaphs

Here lies the body
Of a girl named Emily
She was small
And very smelly!

Phoebe Hack (8)
Brookland Junior School

The Quest

Brave, clever and strong,
Old as Earth,
Ducking and jumping to move on,
Completing impossible tasks.

Old deserted temple,
Small outside,
Huge inside,
On a cliff,
Sea waves rough as a carpet.

Brave, clever and strong,
Old as Earth,
Ducking and jumping to move on,
Completing impossible tasks,
Weaker, weaker and weaker,
Fell to the ground,
Stayed as still as rock.

Anthony Weller (11)
Brookland Junior School

My Pet

My pet is brown and sweet
My pet loves to eat
My pet has a tail
My pet is very neat
My pet loves cheese
My pet lives in a house
For my pet is a tiny, wiry, trouble making, cute and cuddly . . .

Nicola Isaacs (9)
Brookland Junior School

The Demon

He stood stock still,
Eyes darker than ebony,
Skin crimson-red,
Horns as sharp as a whetted knife,
He now began to take flight.

His purpose was to slay,
His soul restless until the time came,
He was summoned by a boy,
But knew he had to die,
His name was Balthazar.

His eyes were full of grief,
Raising an ancient hand,
It filled up with his sacred magic,
Blue fire for what it was,
He hurdled it towards the boy,
And Balthazar had slayed once more.

Ivan Georgiev (11)
Brookland Junior School

Magic

The dark cloaked, hooded magician stood,
Waiting,
Waiting at the edge of the cliff,
And out of nowhere there came,
A short zap from the magician's wand.

Glamorous, shiny and polished.
The magician's dazzling diamond appeared
For the quest that he did the day before.

He picked it up and turned to walk
But stumbled along the way,
He tried to stabilize himself but couldn't
He slowly fell away that day.

Elise Baker (11)
Brookland Junior School

The Magician

The magician stood stock still
As old as life
Ruby-red eyes
The magician was eternal life.

Many magical doors
One was life
The others were death
He chose oak
His life was spared.

The dazzling, designed mirrors
Made to make you scared
Tall and wide
Who knew what was hidden inside.

The magical magician was powerful as God found
Inside
Deep, deep inside
And was only a little boy.

Jordan Elderton (11)
Brookland Junior School

The Who's Who Of The Horrible House

An annoying awful anteater answering
A big black bee bullying
A crazy colourful cat copying
A dopey dizzy Dracula daydreaming
An enormous eerie Emma eating
A fierce frowning Francesca farting
A gigantic green giant gobbling
A hairy humongous horse hovering
An icy indigo igloo imploring.

Emma Saunders (9)
Brookland Junior School

The Quest Of Life

Approaching west exit,
Pondering
Wondering around
Wind biting skin.
Catching sight of a golden arch
Bells ringing
Red beams coming out of nowhere
Ducking, sliding, hopping, jumping.

A room filled with puzzle pieces,
Opening old, brown envelope
Full of instructions
Puzzle of a map to the next level
Diamond dropped from tube
Diamond of life.

People die,
Bad things happen,
Good lasts longer than bad
Diamond of life
Good people live.

Shannon Daly (11)
Brookland Junior School

Emma-Rose Picking her Nose

The chief defect of Emma-Rose
Was sticking her finger right up her nose
And when she sits at the table
Pick, pick, pick goes Emma-Rose as she is able.

Jessica Goodman (9)
Brookland Junior School

The Who's Who Of The Horrible House

An awful angry anteater
A big blue bat bouncing
A crafty cool cat cackling
A dozy dopey dog decomposing
An enormous electric elephant electrifying
A freaky famous Frankenstein flying
A gruesome ginormous ghost growing
A haunted horrible hag howling
An insane indigo imp ironing
A jumpy jade jackal juggling
A kinky king kangaroo knitting
A loony loser leprechaun laughing
A mouldy monstrous monster moaning.

Georgia Pitkin (9)
Brookland Junior School

The Haunted House

The haunted house
There is a mouse
And a bat
With a gnat.
There is a ghost
Who always boasts
Who sent a letter to the queen
Who liked beans
Who liked spleens
Who was mean.

Gemma Shipway (8)
Brookland Junior School

Going Away

It was an ordinary afternoon
Sitting in the living room
When a loud and whirring
Whistling sound brought
Doodlebugs to the ground
Dust and smoke that made me
Choke came flying through the air
Where buildings stood and families lived
Are now all cold and bare.

I got on the train
My heart in loads of pain
Was I going to a nice place?
Would my family ever be dead
Like that girl's in the book I read.
When I got there we sat in the hall
Then a lady came and took us to Poole.

Amber Forrow (7)
Brookland Junior School

Epitaphs

Here lies the body
Of an overgrown cat
He ate too much food
And then got fat.

Here lies the body
Of a wet cat
He jumped out of a boat
And that was that.

Here lies the body
Of alien the rat
He ran out of his cage
And got chased by a cat.

Louise Dunn (9)
Brookland Junior School

Going Away

I'm going away somewhere,
Leave my family I wouldn't dare,
Holding my suitcase very hard,
With all my treasure right inside.
A teddy, some blankets and a few clothes
That's all I needed for the war time.

James Perfect (7)
Brookland Junior School

My Pet

My pet has a tail
My pet doesn't fly or sing
My pet bites my football
My pet likes to jog
For my pet is a cheeky, sneaky, barking, larking . . .

Harry McLaren (8)
Brookland Junior School

My Pet

My pet doesn't shout
My pet isn't a male
My pet doesn't have whiskers
My pet doesn't have scales
My pet chews a log
My pet rhymes with frog
For my pet is a lazy, crazy, naughty, nibbly . . .

Tom Thurlow (7)
Brookland Junior School

My Pet

My pet doesn't have scales
My pet's got a tail
My pet doesn't have wings
My pet doesn't sing
My pet is lazy
My pet has a lovely habit
For my pet is a jumpy, lumpy, cute and cuddly . . .

Danielle Fitzgerald (9)
Brookland Junior School

My Pet

My pet has a tail
My pet likes mud
My pet is very fat
My pet drinks out of a tub
My pet is pink
My pet likes to dig
For my pet is a funny bunny, trouble making, cute and cuddly . . .

Paris Lewis (9)
Brookland Junior School

My Pet

My pet hasn't got a tail
My pet has fins
My pet is gigantic
My pet likes to win
My pet is a good swimmer
My pet is not a snail
For my pet is not furry, nor purrs, but is trouble making . . .

Bradley Hoskin (8)
Brookland Junior School

My Pet

My pet has a tail
My pet doesn't look pale
My pet loves sheets
My pet can eat
My pet is very neat
My pet plays with a log
For my pet is a furry, curly, trouble making, cute and cuddly . . .

Emma Payne (9)
Brookland Junior School

My Pet

My pet does have whiskers
My pet can't swim
My pet can run
My pet is dim
My pet is big
My pet eats rats
For my pet is a furry, purry, trouble making, cute and cuddly . . .

Roberto Catarinicchia (9)
Brookland Junior School

My Pet

My pet has a tail
My pet doesn't have scales
My pet has whiskers
My pet wails
My pet is furry
My pet likes running in fog
For my pet is a crazy, lazy, trouble making, cute and cuddly . . .

Laura Newby (9)
Brookland Junior School

Acrostic Poems

S miling
P onies
R unning
I n
N ew
G rass

S miling
U ncles
M issing
M ary
E ating
R aspberries

A untie
U landie
T aught
U ncle
M artin
N ames

W hales
I n
N orth
T urkey
E ating
R adishes.

Megan Sprake (9)
Brookland Junior School

Epitaphs

Here lies the body
Of a very slow slug
Who was very silly
And went down the plug.

Rosie Sperrin (9)
Brookland Junior School

My Pet

My pet has no scales
My pet is fat
My pet has small eyes
My pet doesn't like a pat
My pet is not called Buster
For my pet is a small, cool, funny animal, cute and cuddly . . .

Jason Bull (9)
Brookland Junior School

My Pet

My pet doesn't have a tail
My pet has got short legs
My pet doesn't fly
My pet plays with pegs
My pet is brown
My pet rhymes with funky
For my pet is a swinging, flinging, trouble making, cute and cuddly . . .

Antony Hughes (9)
Brookland Junior School

My Pet

My pet doesn't have fins
My pet has a tail
My pet has teeth
My pet is an overgrown female
My pet is furry
My pet likes a frog
For my pet is a furry, curly, cute and cuddly . . .

Bliss O'Dea (9)
Brookland Junior School

Going Away

I travel away.
I hope I am going to a good place,
I can hear crying and moaning,
Hissing of steam, whistles and waving.

I feel.
I feel petrified, like I am going to explode.
I feel happy and sad together,
I feel like I am going to cry for my mum and dad.
My mum felt really sad for leaving me,
Because I was gong to a stranger's house.

I can see.
I can see children crying and cuddling their mums and dads.
I can see school teachers with classes,
I can see other children with name tags on.

I miss you very much.

Ellie Finch (8)
Brookland Junior School

My Pet

My pet does have teeth
My pet doesn't have scales
My pet has whiskers
My pet isn't from Wales
My pet is playful
My pet isn't a frog
For my pet is a mad, sad, cute and cuddly . . .

Conor Ward (9)
Brookland Junior School

My Pet

My pet can fly
My pet hasn't got ears
My pet is furry
My pet has lots of ears
My pet has a beak
My pet is not a nerd
For my pet is a flutey, beauty, chirpy and cute . . .

Emily Buckland (9)
Brookland Junior School

Under Da Sea

Fishes under da sea
Fins flickering all around me
Dolphins jumping, *splish, splash, splosh*
Lobsters *clap clap.*
Crabs *snap snap.*
Octopus *nap nap*
Then tentacles *rap rap.*

Eleni Zachariou (8)
Bushey Manor Junior School

The Stink Bomb War

Stink bombs flying around like crazy,
People crying like a baby,
The president steps out of his house and gets shot in the mouth,
He chokes and dies, RIP goodbye President,
Up into Heaven he goes without his two little toes!

Max Wolf (7)
Bushey Manor Junior School

Crazy Aliens

In the middle of the day,
We see their way.
We know they're in space,
Doing their race.
For all that we know,
They will make us blow.

Now we can see,
What they do to me.
Up in the sky,
They will fly.
Then they come down,
While they're upside down.

They are dumb,
So watch out when they come!
They will bend,
At the end.
Which is the slimiest of all,
Or will they just fall?

Michael Hague (8)
Bushey Manor Junior School

Annabelle's Defect

Annabelle's nails were badly bitten,
It was a habit with which she was smitten.
One day she bit a nail too far,
She was rushed to the hospital,
(You see they didn't have a car.)
Annabelle was extremely sick,
And had no nails left to pick.
A nail had punctured her heart,
The doctor said it had been split apart.
For days and days she lay in bed,
A few weeks later she was dead!

Kirsty Henley-Washford (9)
Bushey Manor Junior School

World War II

I can see . . .
Families running for their lives.
Hitler's army firing down countless bombs in rhyme.
Women blinding down their windows.
Air raid wardens telling everyone it's time.

I can see . . .
Burning dread against Hitler and his army.
My bleeding hand, stinging now, the pain is seeping through.
The sadness of my father's death and wished he was home too.
The happiness of the war to end, but still I have to wait until it ends.

I can hear . . .
The deafening screams of passers by.
The halt of a surprised car.
The crashes of a falling bomb.
The almighty air raid warning.

Alice Houbart (9)
Bushey Manor Junior School

World War II

As the whizzing starts to stop
The bomb falls and makes a very big plop.
Screaming parents start to yell
As if they're not very well.
Smashing noises reach our ears
As wealthy people fall off piers
Bullets shooting people dead
When one soldier's lying in bed.
As a bomb falls on his house
He blows up just like a mouse.
A woman called Tracy Blake
Walks out with a rake.
She smashes a helicopter flat
And then she turned into a cat.

Jacob Chase-Roberts (8)
Bushey Manor Junior School

The Register

'Queen?'
'I own my own land Miss!'

'Wayne Rooney?'
'I scored a goal Miss!'

'Elvis Presley?'
'Uh Miss!'

'Mickey Mouse?'
'Like some cheese Miss!'

'Miss Whitney?'
'Canada Miss!'

'Kris Rogero?'
'Funny Miss!'

'Harry Potter?'
'Where's my broom Miss?'

'James Bond?'
'007 Miss!'

'Bart?'
'Eat my shorts Miss!'

'King Henry?'
'I want a divorce Miss!'

Rosie Durant (9)
Bushey Manor Junior School

Poem With Adjectives

On my way to school I saw a little puppy
It was a Dalmatian
It was an angry Dalmatian
It was an angry, ugly Dalmatian
It was an angry, ugly, hungry Dalmatian
It was an angry, ugly, hungry, wild Dalmatian and it ate me up!

Emily Grieve (9)
Bushey Manor Junior School

Ancient Egypt

Pharaohs gleaming
Always scheming
Glinting in the sun
People praying
Children playing
Dancing, dancing to a song.

Soft sand falling
Sun is boiling
Need somewhere to cool down
See a pharaoh
Handsome fellow
Wearing his golden crown.

People praying
Cattle laying
Settling to sleep
I'm the last and lonely one
Except the one who herds the sheep.

Eve Anglesey (10)
Bushey Manor Junior School

The Pharaoh's Pyramid

People moving a heavy block,
Leaders shouting orders,
Two blocks giving a loud knock,
Building the pharaoh's pyramid.

The hot dust blowing in your face,
The strain of a heavy block,
The mosquitoes giving chase,
The bite of the mean flies.

Servants dream of wonderful freedom,
Pharaoh dreams of a tall pyramid,
Leaders dream of a reward,
All dreaming of something special.

Louise Warren (10)
Bushey Manor Junior School

World War II

People are scared and panicking,
Soldiers are frightened and running,
Shops and houses exploding,
People suffering and dying,
Everyone is dying, crying,
Not knowing what to do.

Planes are soaring,
Engines are roaring,
There's rationing around,
My arms are aching
My heart is racing,
Make this war stop.

The heat of bombs turn to flames,
As I run around London I see the Thames,
I see dead people inside its watery depths,
I'm feeling so scared,
I need some help,
This is a never-ending war.

Natalia Cordeiro (10)
Bushey Manor Junior School

Ancient Egypt

Blazing hot sun,
Slaves being whipped for fun,
People praying,
Children playing.

Sand on my feet,
Sun on my back,
Breeze on my face,
Pharaoh glides down the steps with grace.

Baaa of the sheep in the shepherd's field,
Slaves forever yield,
Chatter of the people all around,
Rustle of the leaves that make hardly a sound.

Anna Chase-Roberts (10)
Bushey Manor Junior School

Song Of War

Rat-a-tat-tat! The machine guns fire,
Faster than Concorde, more deadly than fire.
Men fall like skittles, the Germans advance,
The screams, yells and bellows and shots make me blanch.
But I have to stay in this cold, smelly trench,
With no hope of fleeing, enduring the stench.

The bombers fly into position,
Fighters fly up in defence.
The German flag on the division,
Is pock-marked and riddled with lead.
But I sit in this stinking trench,
With bombs falling round me, enduring the stench.

Boom! Boom! Boom! The bazookas spit,
Men fall on their faces, all covered in grit.
Rifles report in sun, snow and sleet
But all the soldiers want are good things to eat.
And I still sit in this stone-cold tomb,
With rats all around me, plunged into gloom.

James Bernays (10)
Bushey Manor Junior School

WWII

Badly burnt destroyed houses
German planes are flying
Good men set for dying
Machine guns shooting madly.

People feel horrible pain
It drives them insane
People feel tremendous heat
There goes some flesh meat.

Then the heavy bombs drop
The destructive guns turn on
There are one-thousand quick deaths
The rampaging planes are gone.

Robbie Gent (9)
Bushey Manor Junior School

My Magic Box
(Based on 'Magic Box' by Kit Wright)

I will put in my box . . .
A pink elephant stomping on the blue patios.
The biggest packet of sour and sugary sweets in the world.
A yellow and orange striped tiger on a gold and silver tree.

I will put in my box . . .
A seventy-one-year-old lady who looks twenty-eight.
A monkey with purple and pink hair.
A snake with legs.

I will put into my box . . .
The sound of glass breaking.
The sound of a cat scratching.
The sound of ice cracking.

My box is fashioned from cold ice with white glitter on top
And a frosty edging.

Ellie-May O'Keefe (9)
Bushey Manor Junior School

A Poem To Be Spoken Quietly

It was so quiet that I heard
The gentle wind blow side to side on the tall autumn trees . . .

It was so calm that I heard
The group of smooth feathered birds tweeting high up in the sky . . .

It was so untroubled that I heard
The shiny water drip from the silver sparkling tap . . .

Leanna Joyce (8)
Bushey Manor Junior School

World War II

What can you see?
Bombs flying
People dying
People screaming
People crying
People running away from bombs exploding.

What can you feel?
I can feel vibrations of bombs dropping
I can feel my body shaking
I can feel the heat from houses on fire
I can feel a breeze trickling down my neck
My heart pumping with fear.

What can you hear?
People falling
People screaming
Wood burning
Engines roaring
Houses being destroyed.

Olivia Frinton (9)
Bushey Manor Junior School

On My Way To School

On my way to school I saw a cockroach
It was a giant cockroach
It was a pink giant cockroach
It was a two-headed, pink, giant cockroach
It was a French, two-headed, pink, giant cockroach
It was a crazy, French, two-headed, pink, giant cockroach
And it was playing Star Wars with its friend.

Keelan Naidoo (9)
Bushey Manor Junior School

Forgotten Unforgotten

Best unforgotten:
My cat's cute purr
My teacher's happy face
My mum's caring hugs
My dad's clever brain
My grandma's delicious food
My brother's nice smile
My best friend's funny spirit.

Best forgotten:
My cat's smelly food
My teacher's shouting voice,
My mum's smelly socks,
My dad's boring TV,
My grandma's annoying rules,
My brother's silly toys,
My best friend's rude jokes.

Oron Sheldon (8)
Bushey Manor Junior School

Oliver Who Sucked His Thumb

Oliver's defect was sucking his thumb,
Soon that defect overcame his mum.
His teeth stuck out, then he got ears,
Then his mum, said, 'Have no fears!'
He slowly turned into a rabbit,
So much for his bad habit!
Don't do that, suck your thumb I mean,
Or else you'll end up like you've seen.

Alan Sutch (9)
Bushey Manor Junior School

My Family Of Best Remembered And Best Forgotten

Best remembered:
My brother's laugh
My dad's happy voice
My mum's happy smile
My brother's small feet
My grandad's water painting
My nan's love
My cousin's bike
My uncle's motorbike.

Best forgotten:
My brother's cry
My mum's shouting voice
My dad's working away
My nan's classical music
My grandad's boring programmes
My brother's smelly nappies
My uncle living in Thailand.

Owen Scully (9)
Bushey Manor Junior School

Edna And Her Thumb

Edna sucked her thumb.
It became too much for Mum.
Soon in sight was a boil
That she hid under a piece of foil.
Edna wasn't too proud,
And then once scream out loud, *'Argh!'*
And that's all we heard of her,
Now it's only the cat's sad purr.

Charlotte Liebling (9)
Bushey Manor Junior School

World War II

What can you see?
I can see children screaming.
Germans and English chasing one another.
Everyone is dreaming.
We are all separated from each other.

What can you feel?
I can feel the vibrations on the ground.
I feel scared of the bombs.
I hate the horrible sound.
I don't like the feeling at all.

What can you hear?
I can hear planes soaring
I think they are on top of me.
Engines are roaring.
Bombs are exploding because of Germany
Planes crashing because of Germany invading England.

Grace Desney Ellis (9)
Bushey Manor Junior School

Edward's Scabby Habit

Edward was in a mini cab
While he was in there he picked his scab,
After a while it started to bleed
He didn't know he was doing a bad deed,
Next morning there was blood everywhere
But Edward's mum just stood there,
After that Edward's mum started crying
While Edward was slowly dying.

Megan Fitzpatrick (9)
Bushey Manor Junior School

My Magic Box

(Based on 'Magic Box' by Kit Wright)

I will put in the box . . .
A silver ball of glittering crystals
The sophisticated swish of a golden pony's tail.
A small, bouncy springer spaniel.
A ring of all colours of the world.

I will put in the box . . .
The distant smell of Mars.
The most beautiful flower from the core of the Earth.
A magical jar of ointment to make things fly.

My box is fashioned from colourful passionate silks of the world,
Water sprinkling from the corners,
And spotlights of all colours.

I shall play with different types of dogs,
Go to fairgrounds every day
And ride on elephants from Africa.

Emma Mascall (9)
Bushey Manor Junior School

A Poem To Be Spoken Quietly

It was so quiet that I heard
Sparkling raindrops patter on the windowpane . . .

It was so calm I heard
The rustling of a paper bag as it rolled down the cold road . . .

It was so untroubled that I heard
The chirping of a tiny bird . . .

Sarah Sharp (8)
Bushey Manor Junior School

Ant Exterminator

Elizabeth found some spotted ants,
Found out that they matched her pants.
After that she got some rats,
Then she made them look like Bratz.
Then she squashed them in a hat,
Then she put them down her back
And that was the end of that.
After that she got the hat,
Then she squashed the little ants.
After that she got some pants,
Then she put them in the pants.
After that she ate the ants.
After that she went to bed,
All of a sudden she saw some red.
Then she got out of bed,
Then she saw some more red.
After that she pulled the curtain,
Then she fainted, *oh St Jordon!*

Shelby Fowler (9)
Bushey Manor Junior School

A Poem To Be Spoken Quietly

It was so quiet I heard
The colourful flowers singing in the gentle wind . . .

It was so calm that I heard
The wind whistling through the light green trees . . .

It was so untroubled that I heard
The delicate white birds singing in the sky . . .

Megan Thornton (8)
Bushey Manor Junior School

My Magic Box

(Based on 'Magic Box' by Kit Wright)

I will put in the box . . .
A cute little squeak from a guinea pig.
The jolly bleep from my Tamagotchi.
The smile from a happy toddler.

I will put in the box . . .
A bushy tail from a cute squirrel.
The soft sparkle in St Albans lake.
The glistening petal from a rose.

My box is fashioned from . . .
My secrets hiding in one corner.
Real crystal that sparkles from a mine.
Hung with pieces of gleaming moon rock.

In my box I shall . . .
Surf the web and
Whisper secrets to my friends
And search for clownfish deep down under the sea.

Amy Dolley (9)
Bushey Manor Junior School

Jim The Carrot

Jim wouldn't eat a vegetable
Soon he became very unstable
Then he wouldn't eat a bean
His mum became very mean
Then he turned into a carrot
And got fed to a parrot!

Jerram Counter (8)
Bushey Manor Junior School

My Magic Box

(Based on 'Magic Box' by Kit Wright)

I will put in my box . . .
A whale from the green ocean.
A blue boy from the sun.
A farmer on a hamster.

I will put in my box . . .
A crane from Pluto.
A spaceship from the world.
A blue moon from the ocean.

I will put in my box . . .
African drums from my brain.
A whistle from a lion in a white house.
A sound of a trumpet in the lake!

My box is fashioned from . . .
Steel, hot ice.
Soft monkey skin for my lid.
Tough plastic for my handle.

Louis Evans (9)
Bushey Manor Junior School

What I Saw On My Way To School

On my way to school I saw a tiger
It was a tired tiger
It was a twitching, tired tiger
It was a ticklish, twitching, tired tiger
It was a tall, ticklish, twitching, tired tiger
It was a tame, tall, ticklish, twitching, tired tiger
And it was talking too!

Jake Holmes (9)
Bushey Manor Junior School

Memories!

Best remembered:
My pony's soft nose,
My fish's beautiful colours,
My mum's wonderful kiss goodnight,
My dad's friendly smile,
My brother's sense of humour,
My granny's sleepovers,
My best friend's caring ways.

Best forgotten:
My pony's sharp teeth,
My fish's horrible food smell,
My mum's sore throats,
My dad's smelly feet,
My brother's tormenting me,
My granny's coughing,
My best friend's tantrums.

Olivia Myrtle (9)
Bushey Manor Junior School

A Poem To Be Spoken Quietly

It was so quiet that I heard
A green croaking cricket sing on the bright green grass . . .

It was so calm that I heard
A busy buzzing bee up in the fresh calm air . . .

It was so untroubled that I heard
A green frog chew a juicy fly on a sparkling lily pad . . .

Nathan Foster (8)
Bushey Manor Junior School

Do I Have To Stay?

I've seen the deadly war,
I've seen it up to May,
I've seen people tortured,
So tell me, do I have to stay?

I've heard soldiers groaning,
Dying where they lay,
I've heard people moaning,
So tell me, do I have to stay?

I've felt gross maggots,
Ants in my pants all day,
I've felt bombs dropping,
So tell me, do I have to stay?

I've seen good men dying,
I've heard planes on D-Day,
I've felt burning, boiling fires,
For goodness sake, can I go away?

Leo Jurascheck (10)
Bushey Manor Junior School

The Basketball King

I never pass to the other team!
I never drop the ball.
I never lose the ball.
I never lose the game.
I'm never a bad player.
I never let my team down.

Natalie Barton (8)
Bushey Manor Junior School

Summer

Sun-shiner
Fun-bringer
Chocolate-melter
Flower-grower.

Tan-maker
Body-baker
Shadow-bringer
Pool-swimmer.

Skin-peeler
Feet-warmer
Wasp-bringer
Honey-maker.

Shade-needer
Water-drinker
Beach-goer
Autumn-bringer.

Marium Hamid-Chohan (8)
Bushey Manor Junior School

A Poem To Be Spoken Quietly

It was so quiet that I heard
The leaves rustling in the sky . . .

It was so calm that I heard
The cold air blowing on the grassy bank . . .

It was so untroubled that I heard
The smooth pebble drop on the ground . . .

Taylor Cobb (8)
Bushey Manor Junior School

Spring

Winter-ender
Sun-heater
Tree-grower
Green-giver.

Rain-waker
Leaf-bringer
Sun-giver
Grass-maker.

Shadow-ender
Breeze-giver
Flower-bringer
Tree-blower.

Rain-ender
Cloud-clearer
Animal-waker
Fruit-grower.

Marianne Roe (9)
Bushey Manor Junior School

The Tennis Princess

I never miss and never slip.
I never lose, never trip.
I never hit the net.
I never miss a game.
So that's why my name is . . .
Tennis Princess!

Emily Forrester (8)
Bushey Manor Junior School

Spring

Winter-ender
Animal-beginner
Baby-bringer
Flower-grower.

Plants-sprouter
Sun-heater
Sky-warmer
Wind-breaker.

Party-starter
Eggs-giver
Chocolate-eater
Bunny-bouncer.

Shorts-wearer
Tree-shader
Fruit-maker
Heat-shiner.

Kate Good (8)
Bushey Manor Junior School

Mean Homework - Cinquain

Homework
Very boring
Waste of everyone's time
It's like an evil enemy
Awful!

Zacharesh Bingham Thaker (9)
Bushey Manor Junior School

My Magic Box

(Based on 'Magic Box' by Kit Wright)

I will put in the box . . .
A jet-black dog,
A roaring lion,
A purple dragon.

I will put in the box . . .
A red tree,
Planet Earth,
And India.

I will put into the box . . .
An echoing voice,
Fifty Cent's songs,
Akon's cool songs.

My box is fashioned from . . .
Glittering bling,
Cool New York hats
And glittering flames.

Reece Doyle (9)
Bushey Manor Junior School

Best Friends

Smile-maker
Laughter-breaker
Heart-warmer
Hand-helper.

Whisper-speaker
Secret-keeper
Scoubidou-fiddler
Teamwork-bringer.

Stuff-sharer
Problem-solver
Trouble-helper
Homework-hater.

Dare-inventor
Gossip-knower
Phone-ringer
Holiday-lover.

Rachel South (9)
Bushey Manor Junior School

My Magic Box

(Based on 'Magic Box' by Kit Wright)

I will put in the box . . .
A loud, barking dog with brown fur,
A dull, black, screaming cat as loud as a baby's scream,
A leaping elephant, heavy and grey.

I will put in the box . . .
A blue person who wears blue clothes,
The sparkle of the hottest comet,
Popping popcorn that can talk.

My box is fashioned from . . .
Glow in the dark toenails,
All of the jewels in the world,
The black fur of a black fox.

I shall . . .
Swim in the high seas with all types of fishes and sharks.

Jake Simmonds (9)
Bushey Manor Junior School

Hate

Hate is the colour of white, blank and silent,
It sounds like fireworks exploding in your ears,
Hate tastes like a great big fat ball of guilt rushing around inside
your body,
It smells like a smelly sock hovering under your nose,
Hate looks like a slimy wet fish swimming here and there,
It feels like bogies, soft and horrid,
Hate reminds me of a dark and empty room, still and quiet.

Patsy Milligan (11)
Chaulden Junior School

Darkness

Darkness is black, the colour of the midnight sky
Waiting for you to die.
Darkness sounds like the footsteps on a creaky floor,
And then you come face to face with a monster at your door.
Darkness tastes like dripping poison entering your mouth,
Totally paralysed and can't get out.
Darkness smells like an odour of a lion's fresh kill,
The smell of blood runs around your body until you stand very still.
Darkness looks like a never-ending hallway,
Black walls which pound in my head, until you go back to the day.
Darkness feels like you have been put in a dark bag made of denim,
But really it's full of spiders waiting to inject their venom.
Darkness reminds me of being tortured by my bed,
And then telling me soon I will join the dead.

Saraya Bowlzer (11)
Chaulden Junior School

Fun

Fun is yellow and orange mixed like the sun,
Fun sounds like birds singing in the trees.
Fun tastes like sweet foods dipped in creams of chocolate flavour,
Fun smells like roses on a hot summer day.
Fun looks like a bright multicoloured rainbow in a baby blue sky,
Fun feels like a bouncy ball bouncing on my heart.
Fun reminds me of the best days of my life,
Fun also reminds me of playing with my friends.

Jessica Dillon (11)
Chaulden Junior School

Darkness

Darkness is black like the spookiest cave with a vampire bat.
It sounds like the whole world's ending just like that.
It tastes like poison on the back of my tongue on the right.
It smells like a smoky forest after it's been alight.
It looks like thick fog on the coldest day right from the start.
It feels like a big black hole right in your heart.
Darkness reminds me of desperation and loneliness.

Rhianna Wilding (11)
Chaulden Junior School

Darkness

Darkness is black like the night sky
It sounds like a Grim Reaper in the hall of darkness
It tastes like slimy slugs
It smells like a dark room of people
It looks like the empty mind
It reminds me of a dark room - lonely.

George Gomme (11)
Chaulden Junior School

Laughter

Laughter is the colour of the sky
It sounds like people having fun and being happy
It tastes like chocolate melting on your tongue
It smells like flowers in a field
It looks like a great ball of joy above my head
It feels like a towel soft and warm
Laughter reminds me of people playing in the sun.

Courtney Hart (11)
Chaulden Junior School

Love

Love is pink like a warm, cosy, pink room,
It sounds like twinkling in the sky,
It tastes sweet like warm melted chocolate,
It smells like perfume that has been sprayed around,
It looks bright like a hot summer's day,
It feels soft like a furry rug.
Love reminds me of my family and friends.

Carrie-Anne Smith (11)
Chaulden Junior School

Happiness

Happiness is the colour of a rainbow,
It sounds like lots of joyful laughs.
Happiness tastes like a fruit cocktail bursting around your mouth,
It smells like a sweet scent drifting around a room.
Happiness looks like a vase decorated with lots of beautiful flowers,
                                    bright and cheerful,
It feels like a kitten held fragile in your arms.
Happiness reminds me of the times when I have fun.

Poppy Haynes (11)
Chaulden Junior School

Love

Love is a passionate red like ripe strawberries.
It sounds like fireworks popping in the warm night air.
It tastes like sweet popcorn melting in your mouth.
It smells like sunflower perfume, sweet and dreamy.
It looks like Cupid shooting you with a love arrow.
It feels like a warm fluffy pillow ready to hug you.
Love reminds me of my mum who is loving and caring.

Kelly-Ann Walker (11)
Chaulden Junior School

Happiness

Happiness is yellow like the hot blazing sun,
It sounds like cheerful children all having fun.
It tastes like fresh strawberries, juicy and red,
It smells like bright tulips in a flower bed.
It looks like a rainbow all colourful and bright,
It feels like soft feathers, blue, green and white.
Happiness reminds me of happy photographs of my family.

Casey Bird (11)
Chaulden Junior School

Hate

Hate is the colour dark green, like dead leaves on a tree
                                                    drooping down,
It sounds like thunder roaring through your head,
It tastes like raw fish mixed with bitter lemon,
It smells like the smoke of a cigarette,
It looks like steam coming out of your ears, like a steam train,
It feels like a lava-rock burning in your body,
Hate reminds me of a tornado, strong and fierce.

Alice Head (11)
Chaulden Junior School

Love

Love is pink, beautiful and sweet,
Love sounds twinkly, singing loud and high,
Love tastes sugary-sweet like chocolate and strawberries,
Love smells like romantic red roses,
Love looks like bright sparkles flickering,
Love feels like a warm, furry teddy bear,
Love reminds me of people caring for people.

Kristy Hopkins (11)
Chaulden Junior School

Darkness

Darkness is the colour of black like the black hole in space.
Darkness sounds like the Reaper taking you to Hell.
Darkness tastes like blood from a prisoner's mouth.
Darkness smells like a man being torched in a cell.
Darkness looks like a black corridor in the middle of the night.
Darkness feels like your heart has stopped beating.
Darkness reminds me of a murder mystery room
And when my light went out.

Harrison Robb (11)
Chaulden Junior School

Laughter

Laughter is bright, the colour of a summer's day,
It sounds like birds singing in the trees,
It tastes like the lovely chocolate cake my mum bakes,
It feels like a tingling feeling running through my blood,
It looks like snow falling on Christmas Day,
It smells like the flowers in my garden,
Laughter reminds me of someone getting tickled with a feather.

Jasmine Patel (11)
Chaulden Junior School

Darkness

Darkness is the colour of black smoke coming off wet wood on a fire,
It sounds like the walls are closing in before you,
It tastes like a mouse eating poison in its trap,
It smells like burnt food burning away on a BBQ,
It looks like the inside of a dungeon, pitch-black all the time,
It feels like when you're stuck outside in a thunderstorm,
Darkness reminds me of being blindfolded, not seeing anything
                                        but the dark.

Siobhan Keegan (11)
Chaulden Junior School

Laughter

Laughter is yellow because it's bright and shows people's
enjoyment that shines like the sun,
It sounds like an echo of an elephant's scream,
It tastes like the most delicious thing on Earth sizzling
on your tongue,
It smells like fresh filtered water taking your breath away,
It looks like a clown, funny and daft,
It feels like a tarantula crawling up your shoulder,
Laughter reminds me of a peach, being eaten by a toddler.

Rachel Tofield (10)
Chaulden Junior School

Hate

Hate is the colour black mixed with yellow
It sounds like a lightning bolt
It tastes like raw fish with maggots inside
It smells like a field of darkness
It looks like a great big ball of fire
It feels like the screaming hot sun
Hate reminds me of evil.

Alex Radford (11)
Chaulden Junior School

Laughter

Laughter is the colour of yellow just like the bright sun,
It sounds like people being happy,
It tastes like nice chocolate melting in your mouth,
It smells sweet and nice,
It looks like a volcano exploding with smiley faces coming out,
It feels like a soft cuddly bear,
Laughter reminds me of people playing in the sun and having fun.

Helena Simmons (11)
Chaulden Junior School

Fun

Fun is a mixture of all the warm and bouncy colours.
It sounds like robins' singing on an old oak tree branch.
It tastes like warm fudge cake melting in your mouth.
It smells like rich caramel sizzling in a pan.
It looks like a colourful ball-pit waiting to be jumped in.
It feels warm and soft and makes me feel relaxed inside.
Fun reminds me of good memories and dreams.

Andrew Hardwick (11)
Chaulden Junior School

Happiness

Happiness is yellow, like the sun, bright and joyful,
It sounds like a saxophone singing away with no intentions to stop,
It tastes like prawn cocktail crisps fizzing on your tongue,
It smells like a bacon sandwich, fresh and enjoyable,
It looks like a smiling face that always cheers you up,
It feels like a helping hand that picks you up when you're down,
Happiness reminds me of my family,
Who always make me happy!

Billy Stevens (11)
Chaulden Junior School

Love

Love is colourful like a rainbow.
Love sounds like a heart pounding away really fast.
Love sounds like a box of sweets.
Love is a bright day that never dies down.
Love makes you feel all warm and cosy.
Love reminds you of all your friends and family.

Guy Grigsby (10)
Chaulden Junior School

Fun

Fun is pink and yellow.
It sounds like birds singing in the trees,
It tastes like sweet chocolate cake,
It smells like blossoms and roses,
It looks like a rainbow over you,
Fun reminds me of lying in flowers.

Edward Duell (10)
Chaulden Junior School

Laughter

Laughter is the colour of the bright sunny sun.
It sounds like a saxophone playing in the distance.
It tastes like you have just eaten a mint ice cream.
It smells like you've just woken up and your cooked breakfast
                                    is waiting on the table.
It looks like a big red volcano getting ready to explode.
It feels like your mouth is ready to erupt with intensity.
It reminds me of my wonderful saxophone played by me.

Barnaby Brown (11)
Chaulden Junior School

Fear

Fear is black like a bat.
It sounds like a ghost crying.
It tastes like rotting flesh.
It smells like a dead bird.
It feels terrifying like a nightmare.
Fear reminds me of panic when something goes missing.

Nicole Wilks (12)
Chaulden Junior School

Hate

Hate is like red burning rage,
Sounds like lions in the world's smallest cage.
It tastes like a lot of loneliness,
It smells like burnt toast, it looks a mess.
It looks like steam coming from my ears puffing like a steam train,
It's enough to make you go insane.
It reminds me of when someone squeezes roses,
The blood is all over your clothes but they don't care,
They know what pain they're putting me through.
It feels like horrific pain trembling through my body.
But by tomorrow they'll be sorry.

Corrie Seaton (11)
Chaulden Junior School

Fun

Fun is a mixture of pink, yellow and blue,
It sounds like laughter and birds singing
All the church bells are ringing,
It tastes like sweet chocolate melting in my mouth.
Dad's gone to get some more down in the south.
It smells like roses so all the ladies do their poses.
It looks like a rainbow high up in the sky,
With birds singing and they go all shy.
It feels like a big bundle of joy skipping through the park,
It never seems to go dark.
It reminds me of memories I would love to rewind
And see all the people who were really kind.

Tahnee Gavin (11)
Chaulden Junior School

Laughter

Laughter is the colour of the rainbow.
Laughter sounds like a huge crowd of people watching a
sketch show.
Laughter tastes like a bowl of butterscotch so warm and creamy.
Laughter smells like a bowl of rice pudding.
Laughter looks like a pot of gold so shiny but doesn't hurt
when you look into it.
Laughter feels like a piece of silk so soft and smooth,
Laughter reminds me of spring when all the baby animals take
their first step.

Jake Caley (10)
Chaulden Junior School

There's A Tiger Let Loose In The Park!

There's a tiger let loose in the park!
It's sliding down the slide,
It can't do the climbing wall,
But oh well, it's tried!

There's a tiger let loose in the park!
It's doing the monkey bars.
It's going on the seesaw,
And riding the little cars.

There's a tiger let loose in the park!
It's going on the swings
It's spoiling everyone's picnic
And sitting on the horse with wings.

There's a tiger let loose in the park!
Oh why doesn't its owner come?
Here the owner comes at last,
Before it destroys everyone!

Emily Fox (10)
Colney Heath JMI School

The Rugby Match

(Inspired by 'Picnic Time on the M25' by Paul Cookson)

Everybody clap your hands,
Everybody to the stands!
Everybody scream and shout
Lots of people run about!

Wave flags,
Rubbish bags,
Make noise,
Throw toys,
Everybody's at the rugby match!

Both the teams are ready now,
How they'll all fit, I don't know how!
I wonder what the score will be?
Maybe seven to twenty-three!

Wave flags,
Rubbish bags,
Make noise,
Throw toys,
Everybody's at the rugby match!

Olivia Goulding (10)
Colney Heath JMI School

Friends

F riends are funny, friends are fun
R egret it if you say your friends are dumb,
 I f you lose a friend then bad luck
E nd of a friend is really, really tough,
N ever let your friends know your dad's secret stuff.
D ad's will always get you and then tell you off!
S o be friends!

Clara Ryan (9)
Colney Heath JMI School

The Woogooloogoo Island

On the island of Woogooloogoo one day
The Fuzzbuzz and the Wuzzluzz had a fight
It lasted from dawn till night.
With a thump and a bump of a tree stump,
A smash, a bash and a crash,
A flip, a flop and a flap,
A zip, a zop and a zap,
A ping, a pang and a pong
The fight had lasted all night long.
The winner was declared,
Was it the Fuzzbuzz or the Wuzzluzz?
It was too dark to tell!

Alexander Wells (10)
Colney Heath JMI School

Colours

(Inspired by 'The Rainbow Snake' tale)

Green is the colour of grass.
Red is the colour of blood.
Green is the colour of treetops.
Red is the colour of chains.
Green is the colour of table legs.
Silver is the colour of armour.
Brown is the colour of chocolate.
Blue is the colour of the sea.
Brown is the colour of your tea.
Black is the colour of a whip.
Blue is the colour of the sky.
Tobacco is the colour of a pie.
Cream is the colour of a pillow.
Brown is the colour of a chocolate cake.

Zenon Sasiak Rushby (10)
Colney Heath JMI School

School

S is for sums, hard and easy.
C is for classroom where I do my work.
H is for homework when the day is done.
O is for octagon, for maths shapes and sizes.
O is for orange that I eat at break.
L is for lessons that I do at school.

Abbie Fox (9)
Colney Heath JMI School

Grandad Is The One I Love Best!

When I think of you, I hear laughing and fun,
Where you are you will shine like the sun.
When I think of you I hear a melody in my heart that is calm,
Up in Heaven you lay in God's almighty palm.

Your face in the clouds is as tasty as candyfloss,
Up in Heaven nobody can get cross.
The sun is like an immense yellow cake,
The most common place I see your face is in the lake.

You always smell of fresh Cornish air,
I can remember the gel you put in your hair.
I always think back to when we sat in the garden,
And when you taught me to say 'please' and 'pardon'.

I can imagine when you wore your silly hat
Also when we fed Sam the cat.
I always remember you covered in dog hairs
And I love you best when I helped you down the stairs.

I will always have the sight of you in a wheelchair,
Even though you're in Heaven we will always be a pair.
We will always be best friends,
Even when we drove each other round the bend.

Amber Brinson (11)
Eastbrook Primary School

VE Day

People gathering,
People remembering,
Friends reuniting,
For VE Day.

Their tears falling off their pale face,
VE Day will never be forgotten,
For the people who care,
And the people who don't.

They will always be remembered,
The ones alive,
The ones that are dead,
Their remains are remained left.

Remember,
They are heroes,
To all of us,
VE Day,
A day to remember.

Iain Noble (11)
Eastbrook Primary School

In The Sea

Deep down dolphins diving in daylight and dark.
In the distance of the deep blue sea dodging sharks all day long.

Jumping jellyfish jumping around
With the baby squids they are rushing around everywhere!

Turning turtle twirling touching the bottom of the sea.

Swirling sea horse going up and down.
Keeping warm the baby sea horse so it's not cold.

Sharks snapping away sharpening its teeth, eating all day long.

Starfish sliding along the bottom of the sea
Slithering in cold, damp rock pools.

Claire Perreira (9)
Eastbrook Primary School

Thirty Things Found In A Sweetshop

A chocolate bar that was yummy,
A Mars bar so sweet in my tummy,
A packet of Skittles so colourful,
A large Snickers the size of a pair of knickers,
A milk chocolate flavoured lollipop.

A packet of crisps made out of silk,
A Bounty bar with coconut,
A Crunchie snake so snappy,
A KitKat bar very melty,
A packet of teeth and lips
So squishy and squashy.

A packet of crisps so salty,
An ice cream with strawberry sauce and Flake,
A bottle of cola so fizzy up your nose,
A packet of laces so sour,
A packet of Maltesers so big.

A bubblegum to make a big *bang!*
A big sherbet tube that looks like sand,
A long snake of liquorice
A drink of Fanta or Sprite,
Chewits so chewy
Some Smarties so crunchy.

Buttons round like flying saucers,
A rip-roll one metre long,
Millions, so many about a million,
Ribena made out of real Ribena,
A chocolate chip muffin so nice,
A picnic that you eat on a picnic,
A Double Decker you have seen on a double-decker.
And a shopkeeper that will let you pay for all of them.

Demi McGlen (8)
Eastbrook Primary School

Hate

Like a spitfire in the sky,
Like an avalanche under the ground,
Like a stampede here and there,
Like some fireworks everywhere.

Like vomit in your mouth,
Like soggy Brussels sprouts,
Something I wouldn't eat,
Tastes like rotten meat.

I see black when I close my eyes,
Like being in a dark tunnel,
Like all the lights are off,
Dressed up like a Goth.

Like fuming when I'm cross,
Like racing out of control,
Like I can't cease,
For me there's no peace.

Michael Williams (11)
Eastbrook Primary School

Black And White Tiger

I see a black and white tiger, it is moving like a dog.
Hunting for a deer for his empty tummy.
He haunts like a howling dog hungry for his food
Getting ready to pounce and rip flesh and give the deer pain.
Fighting over the deer.
Then one baby tiger rips the deer's nose
And cuddling up to his mother and father night-time falls.
The moon comes out shining bright, watching over everyone,
Sad for the deer to die but happy most of the time
The morning rises, tigers out hunting for more deer.

Shannon Austin (9)
Eastbrook Primary School

Penguins

Penguins are floppy, funny, silly.
All the time they dilly, dally around.
They are covered in the sweet, sweet black.
and the white across their bodies, so sweet.
They walk like a beetle standing up with its arms against it.
Walks like a loony duck.
Swims like a Formula 1
Dolphin entering the race.
Penguins can be loyal, rich, stupid,
loony, snazzy, good-looking, plain ugly, cute, a loyal servant.

Danny Kachouh (10)
Eastbrook Primary School

The Chase

As the dog bounds through the park.
The cat agile and sweet
Smells something not so friendly.
The dog is intrigued by the footprints in the mud.

It realises what this creature is . . . *it's a cat!*
It sprints towards this agile creature,
As the cat notices this, it sprints towards the alleyway.
The dog was much faster and it pounced onto its prey.

Luckily the cat managed to get away and sprints off into the distance.
The dog pursued quickly and managed to catch up,
They were both darting and dodging the bins and bottles that
had fallen over onto the floor.

It caught the cat, and now the cat didn't have a chance.
It was badly injured but luckily enough the dog's owner had caught
the dog before he could do some damage.

Daniel Morrissey (10)
Eastbrook Primary School

Thirty Things Found In A Haunted House

Moving eyes in pictures,
Curtains that look like ghosts,
Chocolate bars that are poison,
Scary writing in the post.
Spider webs on the ceiling,
Bats flying in the sky,
Dried out trees in the garden,
Black cats that can fly.
Things that go *bump* in the night,
People that pretend they are nice,
But really you're in for a fright.
Chickens with bright red eyes,
Screeching screaming noises.
Firework guys,
Blue lights shining,
Dead people in the cemetery,
Someone whining,
Locked up dungeons,
With skeletons inside
Having fun on the slide.
Find out it's a trap for you to drown,
Messing around with the dressing up clothes
Try on a crown,
It will electrocute your head,
It will hurt so much,
That you will need to go to bed.
You will feel a creepy touch,
A four-headed snake,
Lots of scales
Sitting on a rake.

Lois Payne (9)
Eastbrook Primary School

Dragons

Dragons red
Dragons blue
Down the mountain
They'll come for you.

Dragons purple
Dragons pink
All the smoke
Will cause a stink.

Dragons brown
Dragons green
From your homeland
Flames are seen.

Dragons silver
Dragons gold
Knights that slay
Are very bold.

Dragons yellow
Dragons white
If you see one
You'll die of fright.

Dragons black
Dragons grey
Something's wrong
It's sure to say.

Jayson McGlen (11)
Eastbrook Primary School

Unexpected Killer

In the silent meadow, across the river.
A stealthy killer waits.
He's always waiting in any weather,
Just behind the gates.

He moves in closer.
For a better view.
He runs around like a roller coaster,
He sees a tasty ewe.

At the grass the ewe will peck,
The fox wraps its teeth around her neck.

All the other sheep will bleat!
The farmer jumps to his feet.
He'll race to the farmhouse for his gun,
But by now the fox has run.
Once again the fox shall live.

Jack Cooper & Ossie Williams (11)
Eastbrook Primary School

Love Is In The Air

Love is sweet like sugar candy,
Makes you feel happy and dandy,
Love is cosy and warm,
When outside there's a raging storm,
Love is the colour gold,
It's like a small child that you hold,
Love is like a garland of flowers,
They smell just like the rain in April showers.

Emma Gates & Luke Hampton (11)
Eastbrook Primary School

Hate

Sounds like you don't like someone.
You are furious with a person.
You feel like taking your anger out on someone.
Being jealous of someone.
You go hyper.

Hate tastes bitter.
It is nasty and horrible when you're not in control,
You lose your senses.
Smells disgusting, rusty and dirty.

Feels like your head is going to burst.
Reminds you of being angry with someone.
Being jealous. Wanting to hurt someone, bullying someone.

Hate flows in the air like vibration.
Sometimes you're angry and sometimes you're happy.

Aisha Saeed (11)
Eastbrook Primary School

Happiness

It is a hot summer day
Birds are singing.
Children are playing and singing.
Sounds peaceful and beautiful.
Tastes like delicious, scrumptious strawberry ice cream,
Like it is from Heaven.
Smells rich like chocolate bubbly, it is sensational.
It is a soft, smooth feeling, everyone being friendly to each other.
It reminds you of being helpful, kind to other people.

Tara Morrell (11)
Eastbrook Primary School

Mirror Mirror

Mirror mirror by the sink
Tell me what you truly think

Am I short? Perhaps too tall?
Are my ears a bit too small?

Am I fat? Am I thin?
Will I lose or will I win?

Am I weak or super strong?
Is my hair too short or long?

Is my nose exactly right?
Or has it been in a fight

Am I nerdy? Am I cool?
Am I awful? Do I rule?

Am I smart or rather dumb?
Can you say what I'll become?

Am I sweet or do I stink?
Mirror, mirror by the sink.

Kelly-Marie Daly (10) & Fazari Peeraullee (11)
Eastbrook Primary School

Grandad You'll Never Be Forgotten

I'll always remember your smell of coffee
Your aroma of your lovely dog lingering around you.
I will always remember your outrageous scent of
                              burnt-out peppermint tobacco.

Your skin was all wrinkly and rough.
It was always pale brown and had brown moles everywhere.
Your hair was all silky and soft.
Your beautiful rosy red lips were all creased and bumped.

The sound of your voice was as if you were an opera singer.
When you sang to me you always sang happily and jolly.
You always sang posh and your voice always sounded superb.

I will never forget when you were a security guard.
You were always making money for Nan to spend.
I always remember when you showed me your false teeth.
You always had to take the best dog ever out for a walk every day.

You're the best grandad ever and I'll never forget you.
You'll always be in my heart,
I've got a place for you in my heart that will never go away.

Georgie-May Lancashire (11)
Eastbrook Primary School

Madness

Madness is crazy
Like a little daisy.

Madness can be like fire
Like a little liar.

Madness is a killer
Like a boy's name Miller.

Madness is silly
Just like a girl called Milly.

Madness makes the teacher crazy
When she picked a daisy.

Madness gets you in a cell
While you ring the bell.

You can be a bit mad
When you are bad.

Madness is crazy
It's angry and lazy.

Madness makes me drink water
Until quarter-past ten.

Madness is the colour red
It makes you go to bed.

Charley Richardson (9) & Lilymay Vansittart (10)
Eastbrook Primary School

The One I Lost

When I lost my grandad,
I had a strange taste in my mouth that tasted like poison.
My throat was swelling up.
I thought that I was going to cough up blood.
My mouth was getting hotter with anger.
It was as hot as a chilli pepper.

When I lost my grandad,
I couldn't bear it without him.
My heart was thumping harder and harder like a drum.
My blood was bubbling like a boiling cauldron.
I could hear screaming and the noise of bloodhounds in my head.
My stomach had a strange feeling; it felt like it was going to erupt
like a volcano.

When I lost my grandad,
The smell of horrible sewage from the pipes coming up from the
Creaky wooden floorboards which made me feel ill.
Creepy-crawlies crawling through the gaps in the floorboards.
I could smell something rotten but I didn't know what it was.

When I lost my grandad,
I remembered when he and Grandma came to visit
And that he used to cheat when we played cards.
I am so angry because I never got a chance to say goodbye to him.

Daniela Sabella (11)
Eastbrook Primary School

Hope's Poem

My name is Hope,
And I climb loads of rope,
I like wearing shoes,
But all my shoes are covered in goo.

My mummy is the best,
She has a lot of rest,
She is a caring, loving mum,
Who likes to have a lot of fun.

What can I say about my dad,
He is very round and fat,
All he seems to do, is eat and eat
But never looks that neat, neat, neat.

My big sister Demi,
She has a friend called Jerry,
She thinks she is funny,
And she holds her dummy.

My brother Elliot thinks he can dance,
But he hasn't got a chance,
He likes to play football,
And he is running around thinking he is all cool.

Elliot's girlfriend is called Sam,
She runs around the house with a handful of ham,
She's got long brown hair,
And her favourite fruit is a pear.

My dog's called Avi,
He's got a friend named Gavi.
All he ever does is run around going mad,
He usually gets told off because he's being bad.

Hope Moriarty (9)
Eastbrook Primary School

Childhood

I remember the time
When I was five.

I thought I was king
Even though I didn't have a ring.

I had a very chubby face
I still wanted to race.

A year has passed away
It is now May.

When I was six
All I wanted to do was fix.

When I got in the washing machine
I couldn't find the Queen.

I couldn't see over my car
But that didn't stop me getting a par.

In school when I was learning about PE
For some reason the teacher was talking about RE.

I am now seven
It feels like I am in Heaven.

When I fell out of my bed
I hurt the top of my head.

Robbie Bates (10)
Eastbrook Primary School

My Childhood

The days when I was young,
I used to play in the sun.
I used to wear a nappy,
And I was always nice and happy.
My first day at school,
Was not good at all.
I met my best friend Robbie,
And we now share a hobby.
My first teacher was Mrs Wilson,
And my head teacher was Mr Pearson.
I grew up in a flat,
And always wanted a pet cat.
I once went to Spain,
And I was a little pain.
I had a teddy called Scruffy,
And he was nice and puffy.
My childhood was great,
And so is my best mate.

Ian Hardwick (10)
Eastbrook Primary School

A Super Slipper

A feet-lover
A soft-mover
A colourful-designer
A person-attractor
A warmth-giver
A foot-maker
A slip-stopper
A flip-flopper.

Ruqayyah Afzal (11)
Fleetville Junior School

In My Coma

In my coma
All alone
In my world,
No one and nothing to talk to
I'm all alone,
In my world,
Please
Someone bring light to my everlasting darkness!

All alone,
Inside my head,
Thoughts my only friend,
I'm all alone,
In my head,
Please
Someone wake me up!

Caroline Thomas (10)
Fleetville Junior School

Murder Rap

Come on everybody let's hear you clap,
Everyone is doing the murder rap!

People dying in da night and day,
All the kids are too scared to play.

Knives are used too many times,
We'll teach ya a lesson wid dis rhyme.

Stop the killing, stop the pain,
We should stop the drugs and the cocaine.

So how do you like our special rap?
Once again please, clap, clap, clap, clap!

Ben Rodell & Jack Hopkins (11)
Fleetville Junior School

Blood

Blood
It comes from a human body.
Runny, liquidly, thick.
As red as the flesh of a watermelon.
As runny as water.
Like a tunnel of darkness
Blood.
My gateway to Hell.

Samuel Sharp (11)
Fleetville Junior School

Dolphin - Haiku

Like a blue crystal
Swimming through the shiny sea
Leaping through the air.

Chloe Swift (11)
Fleetville Junior School

My Cat Called Paddy

My cat called Paddy he is cool
But sometimes he sends me up the wall.
Although everything I say about him
He doesn't understand, 'cause he is dim.

My cat called Paddy, he is great.
Even though he's dumber than a crate.
But I really love him lots
Despite the fact that he's covered in spots!

My cat called Paddy, yeah he's great!

Philip Ruis (10)
Fleetville Junior School

Here Comes The Robot Army

Here comes the robot army
Although they're very glum
The Commander is barmy
And the Sarge is quite dumb.

They carry large artillery
As they march along the road
They also carry large grenades
Watch out or they'll explode!

They also have night vision,
So don't hide in the dark
Don't hide under the covers
And don't hide in the park.

They travel in UFOs
And go from place to place
They invade every planet
And do not leave a space!

Here comes the robot army
Although they're very glum
The Lieutenant gets in rages
And the others are very dumb.

Kieran Tidball (10)
Fleetville Junior School

The Secret Garden

The secret garden,
It's full of life,
Beautiful, peaceful, bright.
As pretty as a flower,
Like a cauldron of peace.
The secret garden.
My escape from the city.

Hollie Coupar (11)
Fleetville Junior School

Exquisite Bud

Exquisite bud
Your enchanting looks,
Unfurl your precious purple petals,
Like a bed of gloss.

Shona Smith (11)
Fleetville Junior School

Forest

The forest is an enchanting place to be
With a floor coated in leaves crisp and brown
Like a fairy city for all to see
And shadowed places yet to be found
All life is sheltered from the outside world
So no one can discover its secrets
A huge iron tree with all her leaves curled
And covered by all the forest creatures
So calm is the forest and yet so wild
The ancient trees reaching up so high
And the tiny seedlings as the oak tree's child
With the soft sweet sound of the blackbird's cry
The glowing gold of the rising sun
A new day in the forest has just begun!

Gail Coles (11)
Fleetville Junior School

Red Roses

Roses so dark so red,
Like a pool of blood on snow
Roses so delicate.

Levi Gatfield (10)
Fleetville Junior School

Daisy

Delicate, dainty,
Like a sun in a white veil
Resting on a cloud,
Icing on a wedding cake,
A beautiful bridesmaid's dress.

Saoirse Hill (10)
Fleetville Junior School

Waterfall

Waterfalls, natural, foamy, gushing,
Walls of rock, now carved and aged by water,
Like a thunderstorm brewing and rushing,
Something falls in, it's ready for slaughter,
Ripped and torn by a rush of aqua blue,
Hanging branches, watching over nature,
Making sure all traces left without clue,
And that many feel a sense, adventure!
Independent beauty, a danger made,
The water is now crowned with silver foam,
The dangerous mood will stay, not fade,
The water sparkles, just like a glass dome,
Such beauty and honour to see this sight,
And beyond the danger, there is a light.

Laura Paul (11)
Fleetville Junior School

Mice - Haiku

Scampering about
Round ears, long tail, beady eyes
Eating lots of cheese.

Matthew Knight (9)
Fleetville Junior School

Life Of Light
(Inspired by 'The Matchstick Girl' by Hans Christian Anderson)

Darkness was my life
I couldn't sense things around me
I could not smell
I could not see.
That wonderful day
When I met you
My life and world
Of darkness was through.
I saw your smile
I touched your hands
Now all my feelings
Are your fans.
It went from dark to light
It shows how much you can do
All this happened
Because of you!

Claudia Cliffe (11)
Fleetville Junior School

Glistening Snow

The meadow lay glistening,
Like an untouched sea of crystals.
It shone in the morning chill,
And as you walked through it,
It crunched like a tyre against gravel.
It conjured up the image of a sea of white wool,
And frozen air racing past your cheeks.
Snow dripped from the trees,
But disturbed nobody as it gently hit the ground.
Every word you spoke emitted a cloud of icy breath,
Lingering for a moment before it disappeared.
A thin layer of icing sugar covered every branch,
And made you think of sleeping on a feather bed.

Jojo Mills (10)
Fleetville Junior School

The Grim Reaper

A dark-bringer
A life-taker
A hood-wearer
A heart-stopper
A fear-bringer
A death-maker
A life-destroyer
A scythe-carrier.

William Akhurst (11)
Fleetville Junior School

Snake

A fast-springer
A sharp-fanger
A slippery-slitherer
A stealth-killer
A scaly-pattener
A blood-sucker
A neck-wrapper
A venom-spitter.

Jack Hopkins (11)
Fleetville Junior School

An Old Photo

A memory holder
A holiday reminder
A thought finder
A short looker
A tear maker
A happy memory
A life flicker.

Tahiya Khatun (10)
Fleetville Junior School

Old Man From China

There once was an old man from China,
He wasn't a very good climber,
He slipped on a rock,
Which gave him a shock,
And now his skills are much finer.

Stefan Maile (11)
Fleetville Junior School

Lightning

When I start a *tantrum* you don't want to be there
As when I start I *kick* and *punch* everywhere
The ground trembles at the sound of my violence
And then I know everyone begs for silence.
Then comes my mighty breath
Knocking down power lines right and left.
I *destroy* everything in my path
Meaning nobody can laugh.
I *whip* any unexpecting tree.
I have no *mercy* you see
As I am *lightning*, that's me!

Helen Tung Yep (11)
Fleetville Junior School

Black Tulip

The Devil's own plant
An emperor of evil
A demon's great heart!
They're the deadliest flowers
Like a dark magician's cape!

Oliver Grisenthwaite (10)
Fleetville Junior School

Daisies

Daisies are sweet and so bright,
Like the sunshine in the sky,
Daisies are all mine.

Nell Rogers (11)
Fleetville Junior School

The Rainforest

The rainforest is a hot steaming bath.
It sounds like a choir of screaming animals.
The canopy is a sea of green.
Vines hang down like ropes.

The monkey's howl is a war cry.
Gibbons swing from tree to tree like acrobats.
While the parrots shriek their gossip
And the termites build their sand palaces.

The rainforest floors like a paradise of miniature beasts.
The skies are an ocean of blue.
The tropical flowers are beautiful and stunning.
The rainforest is an amazing place!

Frankie Dean (9)
Fleetville Junior School

A Knife

A horrible-stabber
A hard-killer
A life-taker
A human-slayer
A shiny-blader
A spiky-stabber
A sharp-cutter
A big-slicer.

Tevin Charles (11)
Fleetville Junior School

The Willow

Thick green leaves weeping down
Like drool out of a rabid mouth
Its clothes are a thick green gown
Thin wiry branches pointing south
Avoiding a head on glare
No animal finds a home in this
It has no place to spare
And its leaves give you a loving kiss
It lives where there's no competition
Only grass can bear to live
It's like a solo man on a mission
The willow has not much to give
But a trunk's colour agouti and a lot of natural beauty.

Philip Madgwick (11)
Fleetville Junior School

Playing Field

Children running
Footballs flying
Teacher coming
Children tree climbing
Birds swoop over
Grasshoppers squeak
A four-leaved clover
The bird opens its beak
The beautiful golden flower
The tree up in the sky
They grow every hour
And they also grow high
The green paper pinned to the ground
The children running over the mound.

Aisha Khan (10)
Fleetville Junior School

The Playing Field

When the trees leader is angry he makes their branches whip,
The fallen leaves waltz around the ballroom,
Twist, step-ball-change and skip,
When the spotlight is finished they rot into doom.
Mini beasts scurry through the wilderness of grass,
Birds soar through the sky, scouting the palace of play.
You would be attacked if you dared to pass,
If you tried to enter you will find out what they say.
The ripe carpet with petal confetti is sprinkled,
In the morning when the sun has come back from the dark,
The dew flares and gives a silent twinkle,
The morning sound is filled with the song of the lark.
Then the monsters come out to have their play,
Ruining the atmosphere, I wish it would stay.

Nevena Stojkov & Marina Ragusa (10)
Fleetville Junior School

The Sun

The sun is a fireball shining bright,
The sun gives out warmth and light
Although we don't notice it, it is behind the moon
The sun rises high at twelve noon
Without the sun our lives will be dull
The darkness will hurt our precious skull
The light from the sun helps us see
The light of the sun can even help a bee
The sun helps us see how beautiful life is
The sun is a part of photosynthesis
Now you know how important is the sun?
So remember that next time you go out and have fun!

Sophie Kiani (10)
Fleetville Junior School

Miss Muffet And The Spider

Little Miss Georgina Muffet
Sat at her breakfast table
She tried to eat with a lady's grace,
But she was not able.

As Georgina reached across the table
To grab the marmalade,
Her juice was tipped all over her frock
And with a cloth her mum came to her aid.

'Your brand new frock!' her mother cried,
As she mopped up all the drink.
'From now on you'll eat your tea outside!'
Mum said as she put the bowl in the sink.

Little Miss Georgina Muffet stepped out
Into the cool, cool breeze.
Miss G looked down on her lap, and there a spider sat,
And it said, 'Get up again if you please.'

But Miss Muffet was a spiteful child
And demanded why she shouldn't sit down.
'Because,' the little spider cried,
'My family are under your gown!

They are all tiny, not scary and you will squash them flat!
Now Miss I am sure that you don't want that!
Because to be squashed would give them pain . . .
And on your gown there would be a stain.'

Oh, her mother's face if on her dress,
There was another mighty mess!
And oh, her mum's slaps hurt her to the bone
Miss G said bye to the spider and ran all the way home.

Grace Vance (10)
Fleetville Junior School

Frederic And Cederic

When that old man Frederic,
Met up with his old brother Cederic
They jumped on pogo sticks,
Broke down the car they had to fix,
Went around being wild,
And they nearly got trialled,
Sang on stage,
Lost half their wage,
Ran in slow motion,
Put on funny lotion,
When Frederic
Met up with Cederic
That's what they did.

Anna Nayler (10)
Fleetville Junior School

Morning Mist

Morning mist is clinging over the grass
Shining so brightly now night-time has passed.
If you look carefully you may see,
Fairies, elves and sprites, or little pixies.
All night they have been dancing
But now they must be leaving only tiny footprints in the morning dew.
Now put your hand carefully through the shimmering haze,
Can you sense a wonderland, hidden from your gaze?
Listen very hard and maybe you will hear
Singing and dancing of joyfulness and good cheer.
Make haste for the sun is rising
And the creatures will not like you prying
Best to steal away in the morning mist.

Kate Richardson (10)
Fleetville Junior School

A Butterfly

A flower-searcher
A colour-flasher
A two-winger
A nectar-drinker
A patterned-flyer
A beauty-shower
A flutter-byer
A cocoon-breaker.

Jessica Murray (11)
Fleetville Junior School

The Rose

The most divine rose,
Sitting on its ruby throne.
A delicate heart,
A romantic love spiral,
Bursting with lust and glory.

Maria Parikh (11)
Fleetville Junior School

Pixies

Pixies,
Tiny magical creatures.
Sparkly, mischievous, pretty.
Like gems of power,
As small as a butterfly.
I want to fly away with them,
As high as the clouds.
Pixies,
As fragile as a leaf, yet so full of fun.

Harriet Knafler (11)
Fleetville Junior School

The Mummified Boy

The mummified boy
Can't play with his toy
For he is dead
Swallowed some lead
He didn't grow up
Didn't drink out of his cup
He can't lie in his bed
For he is dead.

Cara Lomas (10)
Fleetville Junior School

Sweetshop!

Sweet, sour or sugary
Teeth tremble tragically
Adoring apple angels
Wicked wham wonder
Magical milky Mars
Luscious lime lollies
Gorgeous grape gum
Sweetshop sensation.

Adele Robinson (10)
Fleetville Junior School

The Dancer Of France

There once was a singer from France
Who wanted to learn how to dance
He turned on some rap
And started to tap
Then went round the room with a prance.

Rachael Drane (11)
Fleetville Junior School

Grief

My grief will always last,
Even though it's in the past.
The stone that lies there will stay forever
The day she comes back comes never.
Always to sleep peacefully not just at night
Never to wake to the morning light.
My darling stays under the ground forever
The day she comes back comes never.
RIP lies on her corpse
Sarah comes and Sarah gawps
Her body will stay down there forever
My darling pet, will come back to me never.

Anna Fordham (10)
Fleetville Junior School

Human

A hair-grower
A green-destroyer
A heart-beater
A life-maker
A tree-burner
A life-taker
A weapon-killer
A pet-owner
A house-builder
A limb-mover.

John Clough (10)
Fleetville Junior School

Fleetville

F un and fantastic
L ively
E ducational
E xcellent
T op food
V aluable skills
I nternational learning experience
L ots of laughter every day
L aunching fun into . . .
E veryone!

Isabel Maile (8)
Fleetville Junior School

The Sound Collector At The Safari

(Based on 'The Sound Collector' by Roger McGough)

A stranger appeared this afternoon,
Dressed all in red and black robes,
He put all the sounds in his bag,
And whisked them out of sight.

The crying of the great eagle,
The stamping of the elephants,
The whining of the zebras,
The prowling of the lions.

The licking of the leopards,
The tickling of the cheetah's brain,
The slithering of the snakes.

Dominic Attoh (7)
Gaddesden Row JMI Primary School

The Sound Collector

(Based on 'The Sound Collector' by Roger McGough)

A stranger came to the beach one day
Dressed all in pink and green
Put every sound into a bag
And carried them away.

The squawking of the seagulls
The crashing of the sea
The wailing of the whales
The patting of the spade
The laughing of the children.

The music of the ice cream van
The crunching of the sand
The talking of the people
The engine of the boats.

A stranger came to the beach one day
He didn't leave his name
Left us only silence
Life will never be the same again.

Lucy Hodson (7)
Gaddesden Row JMI Primary School

Sadness

Sadness is blue, like a pet dying and tears coming from your eyes.
It sounds as if you're about to cry out loud.
Sadness tastes like tears coming from your eyes.
It smells like the dead body of a pet.
It reminds me of my fish dying and people calling me names.
It feels like you're going to cry and cry.

Adam Rowland (10)
Gaddesden Row JMI Primary School

The Sound Collector

(Based on 'The Sound Collector' by Roger McGough)

A person came this morning
Dressed all in red and white
He put every sound into a sack
And whisked them out of sight.

The mooing of the cow
The dripping of the tap
The clanking of the trough
The tweeting of the birds

The clicking of the hooves
The rustling of the trees
The buzzing of the bees
The chatting of me!

Kerry Burnage (8)
Gaddesden Row JMI Primary School

Hate

What does it taste like?
It tastes like red dry blood.
What does it sound like?
It sounds like a rhino running at you.
What does it remind you of?
It reminds me of darkness.
What does it feel like?
It feels like death.
What does it smell like?
It smells like a decaying body.

Darren Pike (9)
Gaddesden Row JMI Primary School

The Sound Collector

(Based on 'The Sound Collector' by Roger McGough)

A stranger called this morning
Dressed all in black and white
Put every sound in a bag
And carried them away.

The buzzing of the computer
The squeaking of the chalk
The silence of the rubber
The moaning of the children.

The shouting of the teacher
The flapping of the books
The blowing of the air
The ringing of the fire alarm.

'A stranger called this morning
He did not leave his name
Left us only silence
Life will never be the same'.

Alfie Thackeray (8)
Gaddesden Row JMI Primary School

Jealousy

Jealous is as green as an emerald.
It sounds like moaning and whining.
It reminds me of envious children saying 'He gets that and
                                    I get nothing'.
It tastes like mouldy milk.
It smells like a dead body.
It feels like nobody can hear you and you're being left out.
It looks like a wall that has been vandalised.

Lajor Cole-Etti (11)
Gaddesden Row JMI Primary School

The Sound Collector

(Based on 'The Sound Collector' by Roger McGough)

A stranger came to my school one day
Dressed all in black and white
Put every sound into his bag
And carried them away.

The clicking of the computer
The chatting of the children
The tapping of the pencils
The shouting of the teacher.

The slamming of the door
The ticking of the clock
The whistling of the wind
The flapping of the books.

The dripping of the tap
The clinking of the sharpener
The rustling of the paper
The silence of the rubber.

'A stranger called this morning
He didn't leave his name
Left us only silence
Life will never be the same'.

Ami Johnson (8)
Gaddesden Row JMI Primary School

Young Striker Jack

There was a fit striker called Jack
Who sat on the bench with a cat
He kicked the ball in the air
Which landed on the manager's hair
The manager said, 'Jack, you're getting the sack!'

Jake Brown (9)
Gaddesden Row JMI Primary School

Happiness

Happiness is yellow like a daffodil in the breeze.
It sounds like a laugh on a sunny day.
It reminds me of colourful balloons in the sky.
It tastes like ripe rosy apples being crunched.
It smells like red strawberries in a bowl of sugar.
It feels like my heart beating fast.

Chloe Wheals (8)
Gaddesden Row JMI Primary School

Love

Love is red like a heart
It sounds like soothing music
It reminds me of the calm sea
It tastes like juicy strawberries
It smells like a beautiful rose
It feels soft like a flower petal falling in my hand.

Saffron White (8)
Gaddesden Row JMI Primary School

Happiness

Happiness is orange like the shining sun.
It sounds like children laughing.
It reminds me of the rushing sea.
It tastes like fresh sweet oranges.
It smells like beautiful flowers.
It feels like a tickle in my tummy.

Lily Highfield (10)
Gaddesden Row JMI Primary School

Silence

Silence is grey like a pale corpse.
It sounds like a ghostly screech from a lifeless damsel.
It reminds me of an abandoned jail cell with a body,
                                        deserted and forgotten.
It tastes like poison, an undetected killer.
It feels like the cold, grey Grim Reaper.
Silence smells like venom from a dead snake's fang.

Latir Cole-Etti (11)
Gaddesden Row JMI Primary School

Love

Love is pink like a heart.
It sounds like birds singing in the morning.
It reminds me of a heart pumping in and out.
It tastes like chocolate cake.
It smells like lavender perfume.
It feels like warmth in my heart.

Ellen Holdsworth (9)
Gaddesden Row JMI Primary School

The Toy Car

I am a toy car.
I am dumped in a dustbin bag.
I used to be a bird, zooming across the table.
I used to be a jet when I drove.
I used to be blue.
But now I am dumped in a dustbin bag.

Kieran Chauhan (10)
Roebuck Primary School & Nursery

Go And Draw The Curtains

(Inspired by 'The Door' by Miroslav Holub)

Go and draw the curtains,
Maybe you'll see a road
With cars moving along it.
Or even three trees in a row,
Showing off their blossom.
Maybe you'll see builders
Fixing roadworks.
Or some people getting into their cars.

Go and draw the curtains.
Maybe you'll see another set of curtains.
Maybe you'll see a bat,
Red eyes staring straight at you.
Maybe you'll see your best friend
Waving to you,
Or you might see that your parents have barred off your window.

Go and draw the curtains.
Maybe you'll see a dinosaur
Rampaging around for its food.
Maybe a rainforest
Dripping wet and hot,
Or even a million lights,
Blinding you as soon as you draw the curtains.

Go and draw the curtains.

Tom Borcherds (8)
Roebuck Primary School & Nursery

The Bird

I am a bird.
I am sitting in a cage.
I used to soar in the air like a storm-blown leaf and visit flowers.
But now I am sitting in a cage.

Kieran Hanrahan (9)
Roebuck Primary School & Nursery

The Basketball

I am a basketball.
I am bouncing in a bin.
I used to be argued over by the players.
Thrown in the air.
I was like a bird.
I was signed by all the players - they gave me a moustache.
But now I am bouncing in a bin.

Hayley Briars (9)
Roebuck Primary School & Nursery

The Cloud

I am a cloud.
I am changing shape like a smile turning into a frown.
I used to bob and bounce in the sky,
Float and fly,
See people and houses go by,
Cars and buses.
I used to fly alongside aeroplanes.
But now I am changing shape like a smile turning into a frown.

Chloe Emmerson (9)
Roebuck Primary School & Nursery

The Old Car

I am an old car.
I am put in a garage waiting to be used.
I used to drive on the road and swerve out of control around corners,
Like a free falcon swooping down with force.
My owner used to take care of me and drive me everywhere,
Even in the forbidden places.
But now I am put in a garage waiting to be used.

Kieran Hudson (10)
Roebuck Primary School & Nursery

The Gate

(Inspired by 'The Door' by Miroslav Holub)

Go and open the gate.
Maybe you'll see a rosebush
Or a person gardening,
Or even children playing on a slide.

Go and open the gate.
Maybe you'll see a big house with Christmas decorations,
Or maybe you might even see plants with frozen tips.

Go and open the gate.
Maybe you'll get a *fright!*

Chloe Grant (9)
Roebuck Primary School & Nursery

The Unicorn

I am a unicorn.
I am dying out like the dinosaurs.
I used to walk proud and pretty across the plain,
With my head held high,
With my mighty horn,
Trotting across the land, wild and free,
I used to be many a friend, no foe,
But now I am dying out like the dinosaurs.

Penny Johns (9)
Roebuck Primary School & Nursery

Limerick

I was teaching in the old schoolroom,
When a skeleton rode in on a broom.
So I phoned up the zoo,
And showered him with glue,
But he couldn't have been real, I presume.

Aaron Marshall (9)
Roebuck Primary School & Nursery

The Snowman

I am a sparkly snowman.
I am knocked down by a snowplough
And being jumped on by hundreds and thousands of children's feet.
I used to sway from side to side in the air.
I used to stand sparkling like the moonlit river.
I used to stand smiling at all the people who made me.
I learnt a lot about human life and it made me feel all happy inside.
But now I am knocked down by a snowplough
And being jumped on by hundreds and thousands of children's feet.

Stephanie Noble (9)
Roebuck Primary School & Nursery

The Chair

I am a chair.
I am on the bonfire.
I used to be around the dining room table,
Cushioned, cosy and comfortable,
With eyes gleaming up at you saying,
'Sit on me, sit on me, sit on me.'
With ears that have heard a thousand conversations.
But now I am on the bonfire.

Oliver Petts (9)
Roebuck Primary School & Nursery

The Candle

I am a candle.
I am sitting on the shelf.
I used to burn so bright,
Light the way to bed.
And chase away the dark.
But now I am sitting on the shelf.

Megan Ridley (9)
Roebuck Primary School & Nursery

The Paper

I am a piece of paper.
I am gluey and sticky and crinkly.
I used to hang in a frame,
In a gallery,
Shown to lots of people.
But now I am in the bin, gluey and sticky and crinkly.

Luke Thompson (9)
Roebuck Primary School & Nursery

The Fireplace

I am a fireplace.
I am being put out with a bucket of wet water
                                    and being called a freezing fire.
I used to burn all day and night and warm everyone,
Or be lit, happily,
Or watch my sparks fly as I grew bigger and bigger,
Or feel the coal and sticks being thrown onto me -
It felt as though someone was tickling me
As the coal and sticks turned to no more than ashes.
But now I am being put out with a bucket of wet water and
                                    being called a freezing fire.

Kimberley Roberts (9)
Roebuck Primary School & Nursery

The Fat Lady

I am a fat lady.
I am really fat and ugly.
I used to be as pretty as a flower,
A breath of fresh air when I smiled,
Tall, talented and nice.
But now I am really fat and ugly.

Hayley Trudgill (10)
Roebuck Primary School & Nursery

The Old Shoes

I am a pair of old shoes.
I am lying in the bin like yesterday's dinner.
I used to run up and down from the shops like a yo-yo
And go through muddy meadows.
I used to have a cosy little spot in the cupboard, it was like a bed.
Sometimes I used to lie at the bottom of the bed,
Like a pearl lying at the bottom of the ocean.
But now I am lying in the bin like yesterday's dinner.

Georgia Steed   (9)
Roebuck Primary School & Nursery

I Kick A Football

I kick a football.
He headers it back.
I kick a football.
He chests it back.
I kick a football.
He knees it back.
I kick a football.
He kicks it back.
I kick a football . . .
Goal!

Ashley Watson   (10)
Roebuck Primary School & Nursery

The Snowman

I am a snowman.
I am white.
Water drips run down me.
I used to stand tall in the back garden like a tall building in London.
I like being played with, laughter and love,
But now water drips run down me.

Katie White   (9)
Roebuck Primary School & Nursery

Fears Of War In Dunkirk

Loud bangs that hurt our ears
Desperate cries and yells
Fellow mates yell in pain
Of sweat, tears and blood
The shore is full of bloody corpses
Of my friends.

The Luftwaffe crew fly over our heads
Shooting bullets of pain and fear
Rubble hammers hard down on our helmets
Seeing the boats on the horizon brought a smirk
For we were being driven off the shores of Dunkirk
Being pushed back with shell fire
With only a dead corpse for a shield.

Everyone scrambles for the boats
Carrying dead or injured friends
Shooting their own friends to get home safely.
The possibility of getting sunk was almost certain
Across the shore was a boat with bodies scattered around it.
As we left black smoke thickened
I knew we were out of the worst
But more was to come.

Lara Vickers (11)
St John's CE School, Welwyn

Dunkirk

D estroyed
U nhappy faces everywhere
N ever peace
K illed parents leaving children with no homes
I ncomplete families
R ed blood everywhere
K nowing your family might not be alive.

Leah Casey (11)
St John's CE School, Welwyn

A Dead End

Gun fire all around
Bloodshed, death lingers
Ships in the distance
Nazi forces here
Shells exploding.

Kills everyone near
Planes overhead
The end is *here.*
The bodies are still
The end is *near.*
Cavalry is moving
The end is *here.*

Death, destruction
The end has come.

Alex Anderson (11)
St John's CE School, Welwyn

The War Of Dunkirk

It was black everywhere,
People were coughing from the smoke,
There were yellow flashes of gunfire,
I turned to look at my mate and saw the bullet hole in his face.

The bodies of my friends were floating in the sea,
The water turning to red with blood,
The screaming of my fellow soldiers was deafening me,
I could hear the sound of gunfire.

Then the thought hit me,
I might never see my family again,
Please come and save me,
I don't want to die today, not today.

Michael Morgan (11)
St John's CE School, Welwyn

The Dunkirk War

When I went into the battle of Dunkirk,
People were stabbed and shot and bombed,
I looked to the left of me to talk to my brother,
I saw his head lying under a cover.

When we got to our position all I could see,
Were flashing gunshots firing at me,
I saw planes and tanks bombing us,
All of the soldiers were making a fuss.

There were empty gun shells everywhere,
Chopped off arms and pulled out hair,
The soldiers spitting out blood with holes in their necks,
And the sound of thundering bullets.

Wherever I looked there were dead bodies,
I thought I was going to be sick,
It was freezing cold with icy winds,
As well as the thought of death,
That was the one thing I was scared of,
The thought of my body crashing to the ground.

I was very scared because we were cornered on the beach,
I thought we were going to die,
But then in the distance I was glad to see,
The little ships coming to rescue me.

Ryan Bosley (10)
St John's CE School, Welwyn

The Dunkirk War

D ead people everywhere.
U nhappy faces all around me.
N o quiet places I can hear.
K illing innocent people.
I n every family men have gone to war.
R ationing is still going on.
K eeping out of the way of falling bombs.

Megan Jepson (11)
St John's CE School, Welwyn

Die Day

I was in Dunkirk
And the smoke was surrounding me
I could not see a thing
But a few dead bodies in the distance
Lightning was crashing down on the sea
As it began to strike the boats
And as the Germans arrived we began to hide
There were people
Screaming and shouting in agony
People were shouting things for me to do
I radioed the boats to come and collect us
There was no reply for someone to save us

I knew that we were going
to die
So we all decided to risk our lives
to save Dunkirk.

Max Tann (10)
St John's CE School, Welwyn

The Town Of Dunkirk

There is smoke everywhere
With signs covered in dust.
People are crying for their hope and care
Hoping God will trust.
You feel upset and worried
People's faces are all screwed up.
People shouting sorry
With people scared to stop.
I can hear screaming everywhere
With guns banging.
People shoot if they dare
With tanks clanging.

Sophie Hutchinson (11)
St John's CE School, Welwyn

The War Of Dunkirk

If I hadn't been evacuated I would've died!
I was in the sea, I saw blood and I heard bombs and saw
Thompson guns going off!
I could feel the boats below me that were sinking.
I could feel wood.
Thick black smoke.
All around were dead bodies.

Chris Saxby (10)
St John's CE School, Welwyn

Won The War

D ead people on the beach
U nited Kingdom won the war
N oisy bombs
K illed soldier
I can see dead people around me
R ushing to the boats
K illed people on the floor.

Scott Finlay-Nascimento (11)
St John's CE School, Welwyn

Evacuation

E vacuated families.
V ery scared soldiers.
A ttacked by Nazis.
C rying children missing their fathers.
U nknown faces.
A ir force sent to help.
T rouble mothers.
I mpatient loved ones awaiting news.
O ngoing fighting.
N ot to be sure if friends and family are safe!

Indiana Bright (10) & Bethany Rebisz (11)
St John's CE School, Welwyn

Dunkirk

I looked far over sea,
I saw boats lined up,
They were coming for my friends and me,
I finished my salty water in a cup.

I thought of a friend who had died,
He had done that stupid dare,
I had laid down and cried
It really wasn't fair.

I had to run, I had to hide,
I was scared to death,
I was safe, I was inside,
With my good friend Jeff.

I ran outside and into the water,
It may be freezing cold,
But I'd never have manslaughter,
It's better than eating mould.

The Germans were all around,
There was only one way out,
I had to swim to safer ground,
I must never shout.

I swam and swam and swam,
Until I found a boat,
When I got on I said, 'Hey Ma'am.'
She offered me her nice warm coat.

I was going home to my wife,
She was pregnant when I left,
She said I could cut the cord with a knife.
If I'm late I'll be bereft.

I'm going home, I'll live
I brought my wife a French sieve.

Joseph Reason (11)
St John's CE School, Welwyn

Dunkirk

I looked up and saw three figures
They were dressed in black
I looked closer and saw
My wife and kids were back.

I was so happy to see them
But then my heart bled with pain
I realised baby Kitty wasn't there
Then it started to rain.

I asked where she was
They said she drowned in the sea
I cried so hard and wished her back
I wanted her so desperately.

Helen Atkins (10)
St John's CE School, Welwyn

The Battle Of Dunkirk

D ead bodies
U p ahead, the harbour covered in black smoke
N oisy guns coming towards us
K illing innocent people
I njured soldiers
R efusing to give up
K illed soldiers floating around

W orld ruined
A ttacked by Nazis
R eady to fight.

Thomas Johnson (11)
St John's CE School, Welwyn

Dunkirk War

D ead friends floating in the sea
U nnamed bodies
N azis hurting everyone
K illed soldiers everywhere
I nnocent people dying
R uning away from bombs
K eeping hope

W recked ships sinking
A ttacked people
R eally bad injuries.

Francesca Hill (10)
St John's CE School, Welwyn

The Dunkirk Soldier

I was on the very edge of the shore,
The harbour was about a mile away packed with ships,
I could see thick black smoke and big red-hot fires from the bombs.

I could feel the cold wind blowing against me,
I felt cold.
The sea was washing up against my feet.
All I could think about was my family.
I was scared.

I could hear guns going off as well as tanks.
Soldiers were screaming in agony.
I could hear bombs and big loud explosions.

Joe Kleanthous (10)
St John's CE School, Welwyn

Woodland Cinquains

The spring
Baby bird sing
New life brings happiness
Squirrels run wild collecting nuts
Woodland.

Summer
Shining brightly
Tall giant trees thicken
Glistening leaves grow on the trees
Woodland.

Autumn
Crispy brown leaves
Branches die away, *snap*
Small little squirrels hang on trees
Woodland.

Winter
Snowy snowflakes
Icicles hang from trees
Trees are bare, they have lost their leaves
Woodland.

Josh Dobson (11)
St John's RC Primary School, Baldock

The Storm

Here it comes,
There it goes,
The storm is coming everyone knows!

All his wind he makes into a spear
To run us down,
He knows we are here!

As his eyes start to water
It's like a wave crashing down,
It could fill a lake and drown you round!

The crash of his footsteps
Was a sign of no fear
He's here to stay
We better get ready to pray.

He gets ready to pounce
He throws his spear
We get flung around
Like a ride at a fairground.

I think this is the end of our humble town,
As he our enemy,
The storm laughs out loud.
Ha! Ha! Ha!

James Pyrah (11)
St John's RC Primary School, Baldock

Five Beautiful Fields

Five beautiful fields
Stretched out in the sun
A deep scar appears
Like a cat's black tongue.

Four beautiful fields
Stretched in a line
A humongous hole appears
Filled with chlorinated water, kids think is fine.

Three beautiful fields
Lying in a square
Heavy steps stomp
Like a giant going somewhere.

Two beautiful fields
Growing in the sun
A large strip of tarmac comes
As people fly, as going to have fun.

One beautiful field
Lying all alone
How sad it has come to this
What have we done to the animals' home?

Rebecca Jaques (11)
St John's RC Primary School, Baldock

The Seasons Of The Year Cinquains

Springtime
Blooming flowers
Baby deer gallop round
Sun shining bright, warm longer days
New life.

Summer
Trees block the sun
Scouts hiking, dogs barking
Lots of boiling days in the pool
Hot days.

Autumn
Brown leaves fall down
Days grow shorter, colder
Hallowe'en, crunching crackling leaves
Bonfire.

Winter
Snow falling down
Children singing Christmas carols
Having snowball fights, sledging fast
Christmas.

Tamara Luzzeri (11)
St John's RC Primary School, Baldock

Goldilocks And The Three Bears

Goldilocks with golden hair
She has a history of killing bears
She went one day to Bear's village herself,
She jogged the way to keep her health.
Mama bear was bathing,
Papa bear was shaving,
Baby bear was missing,
While Goldilocks was hissing.
Goldilocks went through the woods
When suddenly appeared Miss Riding Hood's hood,
That's a clue, she had thought,
So she carried on with her walk.
Finally she found the hut,
Where all of the windows were tightly shut.
She opened the windows to get fresh air,
Then she saw the breakfast for the three bears.
She took off her shoes, went upstairs,
Saw all three of the bears.
I'll ring Miss Riding Hood; she'll know what to do
'Hello,' she said, 'who is this?'
'It's me, I need help.'
'Oh yes of course,' Red Riding replied.
'My hair is wet, I'll be there when it's dried.'
Miss Riding Hood came, saw the skin
'Oh no my coat will be ever so thin.'
Bang, bang, bang! The bears are dead
'Oh my gosh,' Goldilocks said.

Danielle Fidock (10)
St John's RC Primary School, Baldock

Five Pretty Fields

Five pretty fields
Then a sudden roar
The digger dug a hole
Then there were four.

Four pretty fields
So lovely and free
Rubbish turned one opposite
Then there were three.

Three pretty fields
Under the sky so blue
In came the builders
Then there were two.

Two pretty fields
Staring at the sun
They needed a place to play
Then there was one.

One lonely field
He's the only one
In came the monsters
Flying to the sun.

No pretty fields
Staring at the sun
Only places people go
What's the world become?

Michael Gallagher (11)
St John's RC Primary School, Baldock

The Box

It was when the box came
We were arousing suspicion.
So we had a look inside
And saw micro organisms.
They shot up like bullets
And snatched my pen away.
So we all whispered,
'Would you like to stay?'
So their squeaky voice said,
'Sorry we must go away.'
We all sat back down
And watched them fly away
One of us cried, 'I miss them!'
Then we called it a day.

Alex Adams (10)
St John's RC Primary School, Baldock

Shimmery Shell

It's oval,
And it has little holes.
On the outside it's rough,
And tough.
But on the inside it's shining aqua,
With a touch of pink
And a touch of purple.
It makes me happy,
It makes me tingle,
It swishes in a wave,
And then it reflects.
It is really a beautiful thing,
The shimmery shell.

Jasmine Clive (10)
St John's RC Primary School, Baldock

My Kitten

I have a cat called Ozzy, *(miaow)*
Who is very mad.
He jumps across the room
But he isn't that bad.
He slides across the room, *(whee)*
He scratches the door, *(scratch)*
Then I can't believe what I saw
 Saw him springing about *(spring)*
I saw him do a flip, *(Ahhh!)*
Then my mum came down and it was a complete tip.
She shouted at Ozzy
She shouted at me
Then we had to have our tea
Now that's the end
That was the day
It was very fun
That's what I had to say.

Matthew Duncan (10)
St John's RC Primary School, Baldock

The Questioning

Victim: Why was I bullied?
Bully: Because you were fat.
Victim: Did you know I was going to crack?
Bully: You were so new to the school you knew nothing at all.
Victim: You called me names, it hurt so bad.
Bully: I didn't realise you were going so mad.
Victim: Didn't you think of the feelings I had?
Bully: All I wanted was to make you sad.
Victim: Well you did, but what have you achieved?
Bully: Nothing but grief and fear.

Joshua Clark (11)
St John's RC Primary School, Baldock

The Shining Shell

The shining shell
Has a Playdough smell.
It's shining purple
Like a circle.
It's a dark brown colour
With aqua, green and blue.
It's got a tingly light
With a beautiful shine.
It has effects
With many reflects.
It makes others happy
With an echo effect.
It has swirls
It shines like many pearls.
It is a beautiful shell.

Jamie Barr (10)
St John's RC Primary School, Baldock

Rugby Tour

The shirts are red like flaming fire
And white as the sky.
The crowd is feeling dull and team spirit's high.
Shooting as quick as a gun,
Flying through the posts.
Everyone cheering, 'Hurray!'
That was nearly the end of the day.
That's mostly all I've got to say
But, 'Hurray England won!'

Will Cusack (9)
St John's RC Primary School, Baldock

Football Fever

Competitiveness
The Ref flips the coin,
Blues called heads
Red called tails
It goes to the reds.
Van Nistelrooy passes to Ronaldo
Ronaldo flicks the ball up
It goes to Scholes
Passes to Van Nistelrooy
Smashing volley
What a goal!
And the crowd goes wild
The players felt elated.

Anthony Andrea (9)
St John's RC Primary School, Baldock

Autumn Leaves

Autumn
Autumn shall die
Patterns come from sky high.
Spreading like buzzing bumblebees.

Comes again
Autumn again
Trees are losing beauty
Loving autumn leaves us again.

Once again
Till once again
Come the days of autumn
Again, autumn comes again.

Jamie Cronin (11)
St John's RC Primary School, Baldock

Field Destruction

Five beautiful fields
Stretched out in the sun,
A deep scar appears
Like a cat's black tongue.

Four beautiful fields
With great green bushes swaying in the breeze,
Only to be cut down
And filled with eggs and cheese.

Three beautiful fields
With sun baked turf,
Only to be mowed down
And called the golf time surf.

Two beautiful fields
With birds flying around,
Only to be dug up
And turned to hard ground.

One beautiful field
With sun shining brightly,
Only to be replaced
By factories smoking slightly.

Antony Wilmot (11)
St John's RC Primary School, Baldock

The Seasons Cinquains

Springtime
Flowers blossom
Sunlight splatters all round
Baby eggs hatching, tweet, tweet, tweet
New life.

Summer
Summer sun hot
Flickering rays spreading
Mud turning hard, leaves growing green
Shining.

Autumn
Leaves brown, gold, red
Dropping gently, fall down
Crunching, crackling, crippling
It's dark.

Winter
Snow dripping down
It twinkles just like glass
It settles gently, footsteps crunch
Freezing.

Josh Hargreaves (11)
St John's RC Primary School, Baldock

Seasons Cinquains

The spring,
Baby birds chirp.
Flowers blossom slowly,
Roots burrowing, fighting for life -
New life.

Summer,
Many trees stand.
Small chicks flying around
Enjoying the summer sunshine,
Grazing.

Autumn,
Brown leaves falling,
Trees ready for winter,
The cold wind pauses all wildlife.
Life stops.

Snow falls.
Hibernation,
Many things are dying.
Temperature lowering, quick
Year's end.

Tom O'Brien (11)
St John's RC Primary School, Baldock

Woodland Cinquains

Springtime
Trees grow green leaves
Baby birds sing sweetly
Leaves turn from dull brown to bright green
Springtime.

Summer
Sun shines strongly
Leaves shine brightly in sun
Heat hurtles down warming the earth
Summer.

Autumn
Leaves shrivel up
Animals sleep sweetly
Ground freezes as cold winds approach
Autumn.

Winter
Branches bare - dead
All is silent and still
Living things are hibernating
Winter.

Dominic Louzado (11)
St John's RC Primary School, Baldock

Woodland Life Cinquains

The spring
Sparkling new life
Baby birds sing, buds bloom
Beautiful green leaves start to show
The spring.

Summer
Trees stand proud, tall
Thickening leaves glisten
Sun starts to dusk, autumn has come
Summer.

Autumn
Damp, dark, dull sky
Acorns for sweet squirrels
Crispy leaves so brown - fall by wind
Autumn.

Winter
Now trees so bare
Trees stand lonely, alone
Animals hibernate - silent
No life.

Louisa Halden (11)
St John's RC Primary School, Baldock

Woodland Cinquains

The spring
Sparkling new life
Blossom blooms, many colours
Baby birds cheep at crack of dawn
New life.

Summer
Brings shining lights
Sparkling sunlight dazzles
Children swimming making a splash
Joyful.

Autumn
Leaves start falling
Crisp crunch as people walk
Trees almost bare, shivering cold
Cold air.

Winter
Trees bearing snow
Snow thickens on the ground
Everything dies when winter falls
Freezing.

Deanna Houlding (11)
St John's RC Primary School, Baldock

A Woodland Year Cinquains

The spring
Sparkling new life
Trees gently grow green leaves
Animals wake up from deep sleep
Buds bloom.

Summer
Plants growing wild
Ants harvest grain and seeds
Trees growing tall, foxes venture
Green wood.

Autumn
Crispy leaves fall
Hedgehogs find leafy homes
Trees getting bare, the woodland brown
Colder.

Winter
Snow all around
No leaves left, all is gone
Creatures hibernate, birds fly south
Empty wood.

Emilie Cherry (11)
St John's RC Primary School, Baldock

The Wood's Seasons Cinquains

The spring
Sparkling new life
Trees become colourful
Birds hatch, babies sing, flowers bloom
Trees tall.

Summer
Hot, warm, light days
Light green leaves round
Children laughing, playing, singing
Happy.

Autumn
Dark, shade, light
Birds migrate away
Delighted, golden-brown leaves
Sparkling.

Winter
White crunchy ice
Dark, dull, depressed trees
Bare, tall-standing trees unhappy
White snow.

Sarah Mitchelson (11)
St John's RC Primary School, Baldock

The Skelosaur

Once I met a skelosaur
Who sounded like a wild boar.

It is huge, it is big
It's a hundred times the size of a pig.

The skelosaur is black and white
An awesome beast, a fearsome sight.

The skelosaur eats all in his path
To him this is a great big laugh.

The skelosaur is made of bones
It screeches in amazing tones.

The skelosaur moves like an abandoned ship
But his appearance is a great big tip.

Spots his prey says, 'Hooray'
Once he feeds he walks away.

It smells like a wild pig
But chases after everything.

The skelosaur is a carnivorous predator
It gobbled up the dinosaur senator.

I'm watching it now, it's hunting its prey
Oh no! I'm on the menu, he's looking this way!

Peter De'Ath (9)
St John's RC Primary School, Baldock

The Park

I go to the park every day
When my mum said no
I didn't know what to say.
She could have said . . . um . . .
She could have said . . . anything . . .
But just not *No!*

It's time my mum sees
She can't do this.
The park is something
I am really going to miss!

Bump, creak and *screech* goes the see-saw
Swing, swoosh, clang goes the swing,
Zzzz zoom as the lawnmower cuts the grass
Whee, yeah as the children play
Woof, woof, tweet, tweet as we hear the wildlife and pets play.

It's time my mum sees,
She can't do this.
The park is something,
I am really going to *miss!*

Emma Knowles (10)
St John's RC Primary School, Baldock

In The Land Of The Green Gleecko

In the land of the green gleecko
Blue grass and pink trees grow.
The trees have roots up at the top
And the grass is in the sky, you know.

In the land of the green gleecko
It's as peaceful as cows in grass blue.
You could hear a tiny pin drop
It's the truth, I promise you.

Hark! Here he comes now, *thump, thump!*
The green gleecko coming towards us fast!
Quick! Run away, run away, run away!
Hide until the danger has passed.

The green gleecko himself
Abundant in sunny spots.
Snorting tongues of furnace fire
Snorting enough smoke to cover the world, that's lots!

Greens, yellows, blues, purples
Oranges, violets, vermilions.
He is a total rainbow of colours
Millions, millions, millions.

Dusty as a desert
Hot as lava red.
His two eyes are twin furnaces
And the teeth that bite off your head.

In the land of the green gleecko
Blue grass and pink trees grow.
The trees have roots up at the top
And the grass is in the sky, you know.

Rachel Christie (10)
St John's RC Primary School, Baldock

Spring Fun

A brand new day has come again
Hip, hip, hooray!
The long sweet grass is being cut
As the wind blows it away.
The grass the lambs are eating
Only born yesterday,
Warm and sweet
From head to feet
Only born yesterday.

I go to the park
And have a laugh
With all of my great friends
But then my brother comes along
And drives us round the bend.

Megan McGuiness (10)
St John's RC Primary School, Baldock

My Dog

My dog likes to bark
My dog is like a spark
My dog likes to talk
My dog likes a walk
My dog likes a run
My dog likes his toys
My dog doesn't like a bath
My dog is not soppy
My dog loves rolling in mud
I love my dog.

Chelsea D'Arcy (10)
Sandon JMI School

Street Racing

In the night on the empty street
Lots of fast cars and their drivers meet.
Their stereos blast out fierce tunes
But nobody knows the danger that looms.

Carl and Crash meet and look at the cars
If they win they'll celebrate in the bars.
Their cars are filled with tons of nitrous oxide NOS
They just hope they won't get lost.

They check the route on the GPS
They hope they'll finish before the rest.
If they win they'll get tons of cash
If they lose they'll be treated like trash.

They begin the race super fast
There's no chance of them coming last.
Their cars are pumping out super speed
The speed they need to keep the lead.

Twenty minutes on they cross the line
Crash states 'Victory's mine'
They each get one thousand pounds
Towards the bar they run like hounds.

Jack Squires (11)
Sandon JMI School

Mary

There was a lady called Mary
Who looked like a Christmas fairy.
She always washed up
And would smash the odd cup
But she was good at her work in the dairy.

Hannah Stout (9)
Sandon JMI School

The Roly Poly Tree

The roly poly tree
Started very small
But grew and grew and grew
To be very tall

With apples on one side
And on the other pears
It looked very funny
As the branches all had hairs!

It rolled over one hill
And then tumbled down another
It squashed my poor old granny
And then my little brother!

The roly poly tree
Is very hard to climb
But it is awfully worth it,
For the view is quite sublime!

Hannah Reynolds (9)
Sandon JMI School

My Kitten

My kitten lay on the bed
Resting her sleepy head,
When she goes out to play,
It always is late May.

My kitten's birthday is in June,
Her real name is Lune,
She is my friend,
And will be till the very end.

Meg Lewitt (10)
Sandon JMI School

The Wedding

I went to my sister's wedding
It was something I was dreading
I enjoyed the wedding cake
The olives were a mistake
They made me run to Reading.

Connor D'Arcy (8)
Sandon JMI School

The Fuzzy Buzzy Bee

There was a fuzzy buzzy bee
Who always fancied a pea.
He looked in a hive
And found there were five
So he ate two and saved three.

Danielle Moon (7)
Sandon JMI School

Tiger

There was a tiger named Fred
His baby needed to be fed.
He said to his mate,
'Meet me at the gate
Then we'll give the baby brown bread.'

Faye Piggott (7)
Sandon JMI School

Keith The Shark

There once was a shark named Keith
He swam along brushing his teeth.
He was seventy-three
And king of the sea
He ruled the deep sea beneath.

James Tucker (9)
Sandon JMI School

The Old Man

There was an old man in a tree
At the top he found a key.
He looked down into the pond
And saw that he'd turned blonde
He was so amazed, he ate a bee.

Rachel Croker (9)
Sandon JMI School

The Hairy Kangaroo

There was a long haired kangaroo
He was called Hairy Hullabaloo.
He went to the barber
That was close to the harbour
And fell in the sea so blue.

Alex Close (8)
Sandon JMI School

Football

Football is a brilliant sport
There are great footballers like Boa Morte
There are tons of leagues around the world
Free kicks are best when they are curled

I think the best player around
Is Michael Owen he's best on the ground
David Beckham has had different hairstyles
Having it shaved was wild

I want England to win the cup
Their world rating going up, up, up!
Brazil are the best because they are really good
But England can beat them and I think they should.

I like the premiership the best
For any team it's a great test
My favourite players are Huckerby
And Leon McKenzie.

Callum Thomas (10)
Sandon JMI School

I Love Rugby

I love rugby
I love to play
I hate to be sub
I love to score
I hate to be hurt
I love to win
I hate to be a prop
I love rugby.

Luke Mongston (11)
Sandon JMI School

Fish

There was a naughty bad fish
He lived in a very deep dish.
One day he jumped out
He bellowed a shout
'Oh get me back is my wish!'

Luke Geaves (9)
Sandon JMI School

Hate

Hate is the darkness that lives inside you
The inner fire just waiting
For the moment when you stop holding it in
And unleash it with anger
Waiting always waiting
Hate is your main emotion
Until the light of forgiveness shines on you.

Stefan Norton-Dando (11)
Sheredes Primary School

Chocolate

Chocolate is as sweet as strawberries.
It melts so slowly and softly like a river.
As you bite it the sun splashes out.
Your eyes sparkle.
The sensation is love,
As if the world has started again.
Close your eyes and relax and watch the chocolate melt.

Megan Coleman (11)
Sheredes Primary School

Is The Moon Really Made Of Green Cheese?

Is the moon really made of green cheese?
If it is can I have the shuttle keys?
Aliens running around the moon,
Hoping astronauts will come back soon,
All the other eight planets watching in their places,
The moon staring back at their colourful faces,
Is the moon really made of green cheese?

Hollie Cooksley (10)
Sheredes Primary School

How I Feel About Anger

White hot flames rampaging around a human's soul
Burning and leaving a trail of fierce anger behind,
Your soul changes colour from the palest pink to
The devil colour red of human blood ready to be drunk,
By fierce jungle animals.

They roar around the human's brain sounding like
Thunder constantly banging in your ear
It reminds you of hatred and hatred leads to suffering
Your body has been taken over by anger.

Oliver Moule (10)
Sheredes Primary School

Freedom Fighters

Marching through the deserted town
Hearts beating loud and faster.
An ear-piercing screech,
The ground starts to shake.
A bomb has been dropped,
The fight for freedom has begun.

Max Mayhew (10)
Sheredes Primary School

Despair

Despair is that brown dust that lies
On the streets and the lonely homes of Africa.

Despair is the sound of the parentless children
Hungry . . . thirsty, waiting for their nightmare to come
Just waiting, just lying.

Despair is that sickening smell of the filth and grim
Of the silent night of southern Africa.

Despair is like the gospel grief
Of those poor, poor children crying in pain and hope.

Marc Reed (10)
Sheredes Primary School

An Invitation

(Inspired by the experiences of the passengers on the
'Empire Windrush' in 1948)

It was an invitation.
An invitation to come
Help rebuild the mother country.
An opportunity, an opportunity for everyone, more jobs.
Then back home again in a few years.

I feel sick and I mean sick!
I'll be leaving my friends, my family and even the weather.
Now we're at Tilbury Docks,
I feel nervous,
I have never felt more nervous in my whole entire life.

In our hands we hold British passports.
I thought the journey had ended
But . . . it was just the beginning.
Now this is our home.

Emma Buchanan (11)
Stonehill School

Windrush To Britain

*(Inspired by the experiences of the passengers on the
'Empire Windrush' in 1948)*

I feel sick
I've felt sick before
But not like this.
We're on our way
On our way to England,
To help rebuild her.
I left it all,
All of my friends, my family
But I'll be back,
Back in a few years
They know that and I know that.

We arrived in England
We were shocked, so shocked
The people were so unwelcoming
Looking at us with cold stares like ice.

We won't be back for a while
There is so much work to do
But so little time.

Rhiannon Barry (11)
Stonehill School

It Was The Day

*(Inspired by the experiences of the passengers on the
'Empire Windrush' in 1948)*

It was the day.
The day we would arrive home.
We would rebuild the lost towns and villages.
Money floating from person to person,
Just for three years.

We drifted away from blue skies,
The golden sand and sun.
When we arrived on June 22nd our eyes were fixed.
There were grey skies, grey clouds.
Everyone's faces were dull.
It was like a never-ending nightmare.

We held our British passports,
Our hands were shaking.
We weren't accepted as British citizens.
We couldn't help.
We couldn't help.

Ellen Millar (11)
Stonehill School

The Invitation

*(Inspired by the experiences of the passengers on the
'Empire Windrush' in 1948)*

We have the invitation.
The invitation to help rebuild the mother country.
A chance to support our lives.
A new home, a new start for everyone.

We're not too sure now.
We have left the sunny skies,
The morning breeze,
The singing birds
But now we face
The rain, wind and gloomy stares.

I'm scared, we're all scared,
What will it be like?
Lots of work, food rations,
Any shelters I wonder?

Tao Haskins-Coulter (10)
Stonehill School

Invitation

*(Inspired by the experiences of the passengers on the
'Empire Windrush' in 1948)*

It was an invitation
An invitation to help rebuild the mother country.
The sun leaving behind us.
The grey mist coming toward us closer, closer.
When we got there the cold blooded stares scared us.
It looked like Ancient Greece in ruins.

Aiden Collins (10)
Stonehill School

It Was An Invitation

*(Inspired by the experiences of the passengers on the
'Empire Windrush' in 1948)*

It was an invitation
An invitation to come
Help rebuild the mother country.
It seemed like the right time.
Jobs for all my friends.
We could have an amazing future
Then maybe go back home in a few years.

I left all the shining sun and the spiky palm trees.
I'll miss the coconut milk bedtime drink.
What will Britain be like?
No beaches, no palm trees.
There will be no waves.
No tall homes.

Our ship has arrived at Tilbury Docks.
On June 22nd 1948.
We haven't got any marching bands.
We haven't got a cheering crowd.
Why not?

The smell is awful.
The cold air.
The dry air.
My skin is starting to shrivel.
A lady has just looked at me,
The look she gave me was so nasty.
I feel I could be here for a lifetime, maybe more!

Hannah Daly (11)
Stonehill School

The Invitation

(Inspired by the experiences of the passengers on the
'Empire Windrush' in 1948)

It was an invitation
An invitation to come
Help rebuild the mother country.
I had an opportunity to go with my friends and family.
New jobs await us.
We will be home soon.
I know and so do you too.

We left the lovely sun and blue sky
The beach, sea and the sand.
Then when we arrived at Tilbury Docks
Cold grey stares, stares that were cold as ice.
It was cold and damp when we arrived.

The ship docked on June 22nd 1948
We got our passports out
We were lonely, all hopeless, wanting to go home.

Ashley Castle (10)
Stonehill School

An Invitation

(Inspired by the experiences of the passengers on the 'Empire Windrush' in 1948)

It was an invitation.
An invitation to come and rebuild the mother country.
To give the children a better future.
Stay there for just a few years.
On our way.

We left . . .
We left beautiful skies.
We left the sun, the waves
For the shock of damp and cold.

Waiting on the Empire Windrush
Waiting . . .
Found ourselves on the British Tilbury Docks,
Holding our British passports in our hands.
We only wanted to be here for a few years
But we stayed for a lifetime.

Alex Kelly (11)
Stonehill School

An Invitation

*(Inspired by the experiences of the passengers on the
'Empire Windrush' in 1948)*

An invitation
It was an invitation.
An invitation to come
Help rebuild the mother country.
It seems like the right time,
The right time for an amazing future,
For our children year by year.
Jobs for everyone.

I left it all my friends and family.
I miss them so much - I hope they miss me too,
But I'll be back - back in a few years time.

Our ship has arrived at Tilbury Docks,
On June 22nd 1948.
No welcoming songs, band players.
I was shocked at the dark stares people gave us.

Only a few years on this land
Then back, back to my friends and family.
I can't wait - they can't either, I hope . . .
But hope was lost - our children knew no other
Britain became their home and mine . . . forever.

Tarah Loftman (11)
Stonehill School

An Invitation

*(Inspired by the experiences of the passengers on the
'Empire Windrush' in 1948)*

It was an invitation to come,
An invitation to help rebuild the mother country.
Jobs for everyone.
Something for all.
Children have better futures.

We are on our way,
On our way home.
We had left the great weather, the blue skies, Heaven.
To a grey dull scene, the rain grey faces.

We arrived on June 22nd
No cheerful band to welcome us.
The only sound was the awful coughing,
People crying, rain falling, a replica of Hell.

We stayed for a few years.
We will stay until there is laughter.
Until homes contain a happy family.
Four-hundred and ninety-two workers including myself
Helped to rebuild the happiness.
We thought the end was here.
Little did we know, it had just begun . . . just begun.

Joseph Otway (11)
Stonehill School

The Invitation

(Inspired by the experiences of the passengers on the
'Empire Windrush' in 1948)

It was an invitation.
An invitation to come
Help rebuild the mother country.
It seemed like an open window,
An open window to explore.
A better future
For us, our children and others.
Only here for a few years.
Back home soon,
Soon.

The bright blue skies
Hot beaches,
The happy faces turned to grey skies.
No hot sandy beaches and sharp stares
The ship finally arrived, June 22nd 1948.
Four-hundred and ninety-two cheerfuls stepped ashore.

As we stepped onto the cold concrete path,
Nothing welcomed us, nothing.
It was the complete opposite from a welcome.
We were having second thoughts.
Nobody thought we were British . . . but we were.
They should have been happy the war was over.

Sarah Waldock (11)
Stonehill School

The Mother Country

*(Inspired by the experiences of the passengers on the
'Empire Windrush' in 1948)*

An invitation arrived,
An invitation arrived today.
We are all packed and ready to go,
We're going to rebuild the mother country.
Jobs for you and me,
A crystal clear future for you and me,
But we're on our way back home.

It rocked and shook and splashed,
I'm not sure now.
But it's too late,
Bye to the golden sands and cool coconut milk
And hello to freezing weather.
Hello to no golden sands,
Hello to cold hard stares.
Cold, cold stares.

We got on the port steps,
Evil glares were shot at us.
Pale faces mumbled and groaned,
Eyes followed us everywhere,
Hisses followed also.
Pale faces, mumbling and hissing,
This is home for our children and us,
For a lifetime and more.

Ella Ellisdon (11)
Stonehill School